MW00744580

FROM MAIN ST TO WALL ST
How the Streets of South Central, Los Angeles Shaped the Mind of a
Successful Hedge Fund Executive
©2021, Jeffrey Gonsalves

ISBN: 978-1-09837-002-2
ISBN eBook: 978-1-09837-003-9

JEFFREY GONSALVES

FROM MAIN ST TO WALL ST

How the Streets of South Central, Los Angeles Shaped the Mind of a Successful Hedge Fund Executive

IN 1973 AT THE AGE OF ELEVEN, Lee saw his father Lewis get murdered by a Los Angeles police officer. Three years later, his cousin Tanisha and her six-month-old baby were slaughtered and dumped in the middle of 77th street.

Despite growing up in an environment of police brutality, gangs, and drugs, Lee was able to escape and go to college. He obtained his MBA, then built his own hedge fund company - CYGNUS Investments.

But now everything Lee worked so hard for is in jeopardy. When his friend from college was poisoned to death, it triggered an FBI investigation into securities fraud for Lee's past trading practices. So, the Security Exchange Commission suspended all CYGNUS Investments' account management activities.

Also, Lee's top executive Ashtiyani, donated funds from CYGNUS Investments to an organization that's a front for the terrorist group Hamas and the firm was raided by Homeland Security.

Just when Lee thought things couldn't get any worse, his beloved nephew Jahi went into a coma.

CHAPTER 1

Los Angeles, California 8:07 p.m.

"Boy, gimme that damn gun!"

"I wasn't doin' nothin', I was just lookin' at it."

"Here." Lewis opened the passenger-side door, snatched the black .45 Ruger out of Lee's hand and replaced it with a box of Whoppers. Then he stashed the gun back into the glove compartment and looked around, making sure no one saw.

"Sorry, Dad."

"Just sit back and enjoy the flick."

Fist of Fury was a Bruce Lee movie Lee had been waiting to see ever since he saw the previews. As an only child, he and his father would hang out as much as possible and would go to the drive-in theater once a month. Most of the time, Lewis was either busy working as an electrician or helping organize Black Panther rallies.

A year earlier, when Lee was ten, he found his mother on the bathroom floor with white foam oozing out of the corner's of her mouth, and a needle stuck in her arm. Dead from a heroin overdose.

"Dad, no one can beat Bruce Lee because he trained so hard, hunh?"

"Yeah, and he created his own fighting style. But most importantly, he was able to control his emotions. And that's why I put you in karate classes. You'll learn discipline. We Panthers stress self-sacrifice."

Lee's back straightened.

The movie ended and it was getting late, especially for a school night, and Lewis didn't want a call about Lee falling asleep in class.

They unhooked the movie speakers off the windows and placed them on their stands.

Lewis started the engine of his beige 1972 LTD and reversed out of the slot.

"That man whooped everybody." Lee bounced in the seat, shadow-boxing.

"Yeah, son, that's what I call a baaad man." They both laughed as Lewis pushed an 8- track into the deck to play Marvin Gaye's "Inner City Blues." Lewis's light complexion highlighted his dark afro that glistened from the Soft-N-Sheen from oncoming headlights.

They turned onto Main Street, where a police car was parked on the corner of 77th. As they drove past, the black and white Ford Galaxy began to follow. Lewis kept his eyes on it in the rearview mirror. In no time, the squad car eased so close to the back of the trunk that the reflection from the headlights blinded him. He turned the blinkers on with the pursuing vehicle inches from his LTD bumper.

Red and blue lights flashed without a siren signaling for the car to pull over.

Lewis turned onto a residential street, slowed to a complete stop, and shut off the engine.

Two white male officers stepped out of their vehicle with billy clubs.

Lee looked at his father, eyes wide. "Dad why…" "Son don't say a word and stay in the car."

The officer, whose nametag read McClinsky, approached the driver's side and tapped on the window with his stick.

"Looks like we gotta smartass," McClinsky said in a deep smirking voice across the roof to his partner.

"Is there a problem officer?"

"License and registration!" The burly officer of six feet shone a flashlight in Lewis' face.

The officer on Lee's side of the car was short and stocky with a thin red mustache. Lee saw 'Lynch' on the nametag as he watched the man probe the back seat.

Lewis started to reach for the glove compartment but when he caught Lee's eye, he sat back, then slowly reached into his back pocket for his wallet. "Here you go, sir."

McClinsky snatched the driver's license out of Lewis's hand and barely glanced at it. "Step out of the car, boy!" he growled.

Lewis opened the door so slowly that it creaked. As soon as his left foot touched the street, McClinsky grabbed a fistful of Lewis's shirt.

"Man what the hell!" Lewis spat.

"I said now!" McClinsky yanked Lewis to the ground.

Lewis's palms scraped across the asphalt, peeling skin as he braced for the fall.

McClinsky shoved a knee into Lewis's back and smashed the night stick across the side of his face.

Inhaling the odor of tar and oil, Lewis rolled out of the cop's leverage, shoved him onto his side, and leapt up. He spun around and kicked McClinsky on the side of the head, knocking him against the back of the LTD. Straddling the officer, he began punching the bridge of McClinsky's nose until he heard the bone crack.

Gun drawn, Lynch ran around the front of the car, huffing. Nostrils flared. Eyes narrowed. His aim steady. He squeezed the trigger.

Thunder from the cylinder sent flashes from the barrel. Four shots echoed through the quiet neighborhood to land in Lewis's back.

Lewis's chest heaved from drawn-out, gravely gasps. He turned his head toward Lee and saw tears rolling down his son's cheeks.

Heart pounding and fists clenched, Lee cast a look at the glove compartment, then back at his father.

Lewis's body went limp, and he died in the street.

* * *

The Los Angeles Sheriff's Department completed its investigation of the shooting in less than twenty-four hours. When Lewis and Lee drove past the squad car, police ran the license plate and Lewis's name came back as an LAPD target. This was because of a previous incident that occurred one night at a Black Panther meeting where they were organizing to feed breakfast to the neighborhood children before school. Police arrived using the excuse that they had gotten complaints of loud noises. A confrontation ensued and a few Panthers were taken into custody but released the following morning with minor citations for disorderly conduct.

The night Lewis was shot, a search of the LTD revealed a .45 semi-automatic inside the glove box, which was used to justify the slaughter under the cover of J. Edgar Hoover's counter intelligence program to destroy black nationalism.

CHAPTER 2

It had been three years. The sun was sinking below the city, when Lee and his older cousin Yusuf approached the intersection of 77th and San Pedro. They noticed people from the neighborhood gathering in the street.

A Los Angeles County coroner van was slowly driving through but was blocked. Police were being shoved and cursed at, so they pointed pepper spray at the crowd, and sectioned off an area of the street with yellow tape.

"What the hell's goin' on?" Yusuf said.

"I don't know, let's see what's up."

The two trotted towards the scene, when a loud shriek sent chills down Lee's spine.

"Blood that's my momma!" Yusuf dashed into a sprint. Lee trailed behind him. They zig-zagged through the crowd to the front and saw two men holding Yusuf's mother up by her arms as her knees buckled.

"No, no, no... not my babies!" Ms. Davis wailed.

Yusuf tried to catch his breath. "Momma, what's wrong?"

Two gangsters ducked under the crime scene tape to look under four white blood- soaked sheets spread out in the center of the road and were held at gun point by police.

"They killed my babies!"

Yusuf ran past the officers to the bodies and was immediately wrestled to the ground. His suede burgundy golf cap fell into a pool of blood.

Lee found an investigator who was writing information down on a small note pad. "Detective, who's under those sheets?" The detective glanced at Lee and continued writing. "Aye man, you hear me. Who is layin' in the street?"

A brown-skinned teenage boy, with a low-cut fade, and a blue backpack was standing on the sidewalk. Next to him stood a dark-skinned girl his age wearing pigtails with red barrettes. "Say homie, we saw who it was," the boy said.

Lee walked over to them. "Who was it?"

"Me and my sister was comin' home from school, and seen it was Yusuf's sister and her baby layin' in the street with blood everywhere."

Lee dropped his head. "Damn man, are you sure?"

"Yeah, we sure," the young girl answered.

Yusuf's sister Tanisha was stabbed twenty-seven times, with her throat slashed so deep that she was nearly decapitated. And Mia, her six-month-old, had a telephone cord wrapped around her neck with her arms hacked off and discarded a couple of feet from her infant body. It was a message from a rival gang.

Later that night, after the bodies were taken away, gunshots rang out in urban warfare; the city of Angels' Vietnam. Teams of MAD SWANS were dressed in black, and the Los Angeles police helicopter hovered over the east side of South Central with its spotlight scouring for shooters who used the cover of darkness as camouflage.

Two weeks after the murders in the mid-morning hours, the white wooden church overflowed with people into the street. All the neighborhood gangsters wore crimson red and black, with other Blood sets also paying their respects.

Pastor Brown began his eulogy. "There are too many mothers and grandmothers grieving. In the natural sequence of things, parents should die before their children."

"Speak brotha," the assistant minister said through weeping, moans, and sniffles.

"We have become tribes and clans. Blood is a tribe, Crip is a tribe. But as long as you think like tribes, the true enemy can keep you killing each other, until a leader comes along who makes you able to see each other as one people and not a tribe."

"Preach!" an old heavy-set lady wearing a curly wig shouted. "We don't need any more of our people's blood in the streets." Pastor Brown looked at all the gangsters.

Later that afternoon after the burial, a meeting was held at the recreation center in the neighborhood. All the SWAN BLOODS were present.

"We gone kill them niggas wherever we see 'em. On sight!" O.G. Kapone said.

Yusuf sat quiet, head down, hand behind his neck twirling the end of one of his cornrows around his finger.

"Yeah, and if you see they momma's, grandmomma's or sista's, kill they ass too!" Big

Nutt responded.

No one disagreed. When the meeting concluded everyone knew to create as many funerals as possible.

One night, Lee was at home sitting on the front porch in his aunt Delores' brown wooden rocking chair, brushing the waves in his hair. All the street lights were shot out, and he could barely see the silhouette of someone wearing a U.S. Army baseball cap and a long dark tattered trench coat. He was carrying a handheld shopping basket full of cans walking in Lee's direction. Lee thought it was one of the local homeless men…

"What that S-Gang like Blood!" Yusuf barked.

"Man, what the fuck?!"

Lee noticed a black .44 Magnum hidden under empty cans. Yusuf continued to the back of the house and vanished into the alley.

* * *

Lee's aunt Delores sent him to New Orleans to live with his sister, who was his grandmother, hoping to remove him from the continuous gang violence of South Central. She made Lee vacuum his room and wash dishes every day, and told him that this 'LA' was Louisiana. Indicating, she would not tolerate what he was used to getting away with back in Los Angeles.

Lee's grandmother would wake up every morning at 4:00 a.m., turn on her bedroom lamp, and put on her round bifocals to read her Bible before going into the kitchen to make biscuits, bacon, and eggs. She would always quote Proverbs 9:14: "Wise men layup knowledge: but the mouth of the foolish is near destruction," to Lee.

Everyone called her Lu, which was short for Louise. She was heavy-set, five-foot-four, and her weight shifted from side to side. And when she walked down the hallway the thin floorboards creaked. Her skin was dark from her Nigerian roots and her hair was barely long enough to warp around the pink rollers she wore.

Lee's grandfather Ernest passed away from prostate cancer while Lee was in elementary school, so he didn't remember much about him other than he liked to fish. Louise kept pictures of Ernest in every room of the house with the exception of the bathroom. Ernest wore an afro just like Lee's father did, yet the only difference between the two was that Lee's father had lighter skin.

Louise's house was a small, one-story, tan shack with splintered boards outlining the bottom exterior. The mesh on the front door was fastened in place with bread ties to keep the southern flies out. When it rained, Louise would set pots around the house to catch the water that leaked through the broken sheetrock that expose the molded two-by-fours of the roof.

"Lee Lee," Louise called him.

"Yes, Grandma?"

"Go to da sto' and get me some flour, da money on top of my dressa," she shouted from

the kitchen.

Lee went in her bedroom, swiped the $5 bill off the dresser and went out the door.

While he walked down the cracked street patched with tar, he saw two teenage boys throwing a nerf football back and forth. They were in the front yard next to a pecan tree at a white house that stood on six pillars.

"Hey man, what's yo name?" one of the boys with small plats in his hair, asked. "My name is Lee, what's yours?"

"My name Jaimy and dis my lil' brotha Anthony. You ain't from here hunh?"

"Naw, I'm from California. I just came to live with my grandmother for a little while."

Lee continued to the store.

"Aye Lee, you wanna come wit us?" "Go with you where?"

"To make some money," Anthony chimed in.

Now they had Lee's full attention. "To make some money?" "Yeah," Jaimy said.

"I have to go to the store first, we'll talk when I get back."

Lee hurried the three blocks down the old sidewalk with cement sections pushed out of place by the weeds, to the local corner store. When he got back, he rushed into the house and gave his grandmother the bag of flour. Then went back into her room and tossed four ones and a penny on her dresser before going back outside, where Jaimy and Anthony waited.

"Bout time," Jaimy grinned.

"So how are you gonna make some money?"

"We sell parade necklace jes dat we get off da floats."

"You talkin' about those things made of beads they throw to people for free?" Lee was confused at how those were worth anything.

"Yeah, people pay money fo' those if you have enough of 'em. And I know dis old white voodoo lady dat will pay us fo' some."

"So what do I have to do?"

"Me and my lil brotha just need a look-out while we go through da floats and collect as many as we can."

This sounded simple enough to Lee. Plus, he thought it would be good to give his grandmother some money to help out. "So, where are they?" Lee asked.

"We have to hitch a ride on da trains to get to da warehouse shed where they keep

'em," Jaimy replied.

Lee's eyebrows raised with wrinkles forming on his forehead at the thought of jumping onto a moving train.

"So are you gonna hop da train wit us or what?" Anthony asked. He combed out his hair with the black-power fist pick that was stuck in the top of his mini-afro.

"Okay, let's do it. I'll keep watch for y'all."

"We can get a couple hundred dollars if we can fill up two trash bags. 'Specially if we find any African masks, spears, or doubloons," Jaimy explained.

"Doubloons, what is that?"

"They are coins dat are in different sizes like real money," Anthony said.

The three walked up the street to the levee, in the summers humidity until they arrived at the train tracks alongside the Mississippi River. They followed the tracks to the station where the box cars sprayed with graffiti were parked.

"Come on y'all," Jaimy said. They all started jogging alongside one of the trains heading

for the city of Gretna. Jaimy jumped onto the ladder steps, followed by Anthony and Lee.

After about 20 minutes, the trained slowed, and Jaimy knew they had reached their destination and needed to get off. They all jumped off one by one making sure no one saw them. While they walked down the side of the levee, Lee was irritated by the gnats sticking to the sweat on his skin. He swatted at the swarm. "Goddamn man! These bugs are everywhere."

They finally arrived at a huge warehouse with a barbed wire fence. Jaimy found an area in the corner of the gate that was bent and started pulling it to create an opening. "Help me," he huffed.

Anthony and Lee stuck their fingers through the links and pulled so they could all squeeze through. Once inside, Jaimy led the way around the back of the building as though he knew exactly where to go. They entered through a side door and saw parade floats lined next to each other side by side. Jaimy and Anthony quickly removed the trash bags they had tucked in the front of their shorts and jumped on one.

While Anthony was rummaging through the float, he found what they were looking for. "Ooooh look, there's a lot of beads in here." There were assortments in piles that were sapphire, ruby, and yellow.

"Make sho' no one's comin'," Jaimy told Lee as they tossed necklaces in the bags. The two went through each float until both trash bags were full to where they could barely tie a knot. Once they were done, they hoisted the bags over their shoulders and the two staggered with Lee in front of them. They headed back in the direction from where they had come; hearts pounding, and sweating.

When they returned to the tracks, they saw a train slowly going back to New Orleans. Jaimy began running with Anthony and Lee following. Jaimy threw his bag onto the deck of the box car first and leapt on. Then Anthony tossed his bag to Jaimy so he could jump on next. "Lee, c'mon!" Anthony hollered.

"Hurry up and jump before it speeds up!" Jaimy shouted through loud horns and metal wheels rolling over tracks. They began running faster but as Anthony stretched out his arm to leap onto the rail, the shoestring of his white Chuck Taylor's came untied. When he jumped, he lost his footing.

Anthony's legs dangled. "Aaahh." He tightened his grip around the rail and strained to pull himself up. But his shoestring snagged in the bolts of the wheel. Anthony's palms were slick, and his fingers slipped. He slammed to the ground and the wheel sliced through his left thigh.

Jaimy hopped off the train, nearly twisting his ankle, and ran to his brother lying next to the tracks with blood squirting from his artery. Lee hustled to Anthony and lifted him on his back so they could carry him as they yelled for help. However, their cries were drowned out by the metal clanking from oncoming trains.

Tears glassed Anthony's eyes as he stared at his older brother. "I'm sorr…"

"Shh, don't talk," Jaimy whispered.

"He's losing a lot of blood," Lee said.

"I know, help me carry him to da street," Jaimy sobbed.

The two grunted as they lifted Anthony to carry him down the levee. Anthony's blood was painting the grass burgundy when Jaimy realized he needed to stop the bleeding. They laid Anthony down and Jaimy took off his shirt, wrapping it around Anthony's leg, and tying it with the sleeves. But it was too late. The only sound Anthony made was an exhaled breath, before a slow settling of the chest, then he closed his eyes to the next life.

CHAPTER 3

Yusuf hustled the streets of Los Angeles selling cocaine and marijuana. It was early in the afternoon when he stopped for a drink downtown at the Tascana Wine and Bar before getting on the I-10 on his way to Arizona to find a new supplier. There was a dark brown-skinned man with short hair wearing black loafers, blue jeans, and a white Izod collared shirt, sitting at the counter drinking bourbon. Yusuf sat on a stool next to him. The man's gold diamond clustered Rolex shone brilliantly in the sunlight filtering through the front window. This individual stood out to Yusuf who always had an eye for those who were in the same profession as he was.

"Excuse me, man, that's a nice watch," Yusuf said.

"Thank you, my friend."

"My name is Yusuf, you're not from around here, are you?"

"I'm Chico." The two shook hands. "No, I'm from Cuba, but my people in Florida."

"Nice accent. What brings you to sunny California?"

"Oh, I love L.A. my friend. But I just here on business, I leave in two days."

"I'm on my way out of town myself, I just stopped here to get a drink before I hit the road."

"Where you going?"

"I'm going to Arizona to take care of some business."

Chico called the bartender over, then turned to Yusuf. "What you drink my friend?"

"Any bourbon is cool."

"Two Blanton's bourbon on the rocks," Chico told the bartender.

Yusuf and Chico talked for nearly an hour until it was time for Yusuf to leave. "I have to head out before it gets late."

"Okay my friend, here my number." Chico wrote his pager number on a napkin. "If you ever in Miami call me, okay my friend?"

"I sure will."

The two got up to leave and left tips for the bartender under their empty glasses.

* * *

Chico worked with the Colombian cartel setting up and managing cocaine distribution centers in Miami. He asked Yusuf to fly down to Miami for the Orange Bowl to watch the Nebraska Cornhuskers play the Miami Hurricanes. Once Yusuf arrived in town, Chico gave him a ticket, and they enjoyed the football game. Afterwards, they frequented the many strip clubs on Miami beach. Chico told Yusuf he had a rented boat under an alias so they could sail to Cuba and stay with a relative of his who lived on a small farm in Trinidad. Chico told him from there they would be able to fly into Colombia from a private air strip.

Chico brought Yusuf into the drug trade and they started taking numerous trips to Colombia together. Over the course of a few months,

Yusuf also built separate relationships with cocaine manufacturers and made his own contacts. Chico liked to party too much and it started to interfere with business. Yusuf saw him as a liability so he broke away from him and started brokering deals on his own.

One morning Yusuf emerged from the arrivals lounge at El Dorado International Airport in Bogotá carrying a fake passport from Trinidad, Cuba under the name Omar Cañez. He walked through the parking lot looking for a taxi. When he spotted one, he got in and departed the airport going down ragged streets and dirt trails, to the rural town of Cundina-marca. There was a huge encampment that sat atop a rocky cliff with high walls encircling it and Jeeps drove around its perimeter scouting for any unwanted intruders. The place belonged to Javier Del Castillo.

Javier was the new cartel face on the scene of brutality that existed in the Colombian underworld, where he learned some of the methods of Pablo Escobar of the notorious and bloody Medellín Cartel.

Yusuf had gone into business with Javier, who he had met through an acquaintance. Subsequently, the two began thriving in an operation that ballooned into a 1,000-kilogram a month venture. Yusuf was able to get the pure Colombian cocaine into Miami from Cuba.

One early morning shortly after sunrise, Yusuf's driver was taking a load-car full of kilos from Miami to Fort Lauderdale. He stopped at a gas station along the way to phone in that he was on his way to the drop spot. When the driver hung up the receiver, a gun was pressed against the back of his head with a demand for the car keys. He handed over the keys and the robber jumped in the car and screeched away leaving the smell of burnt rubber.

A black male in his '20s had held up a local convenience store at gun point across the street from the gas station where Yusuf's driver was using the phone. He needed a get-away car because his was blocked in by a supply truck.

The police were in pursuit and a helicopter hovered over the suspect in the load-car that was swerving at high speeds. When he attempted to make a sharp turn, the car skidded out of control and fishtailed. The right side of the car slammed into a telephone pole and the impact threw him against the passenger's-side door knocking him unconscious.

Squad cars surrounded the accident scene, as the police slowly approached the car with weapons drawn. Smoke from the hood obscured the officer's vision as they tactically opened the driver's-side door to secure the suspect. When they pulled him out of the wreckage, they noticed packages wrapped in black tape lodged inside of the broken door panel. The door had bent enough to expose the cocaine.

Yusuf didn't know what to do. He had lost a load and had no idea how he would make up for it. He contemplated going on the run but knew Javier had a long reach and he didn't want to look over his shoulders for the rest of his life. So, he decided to go back to Colombia.

Javier was unaware of the missing kilos when Yusuf arrived and stepped out of the car that parked in front of the camp. The soldiers recognized him when he walked up to the gate and radioed Javier over their Walkie-talkies before allowing him entrance. Once inside, Yusuf's heart pounded knowing he might be in danger of being tortured or killed when he delivered the news.

Yusuf made his way to a private room where Javier was sitting at a desk reading a newspaper. He began explaining to Javier what took place with the load. As Yusuf detailed the events, Javier remained silent and expressionless until he finished the story. Javier then told Yusuf that everyone in his organization has a responsibility and is held accountable. And that he alone was responsible for the loss of $5 million dollars and would not be allowed to leave until the money was paid.

Over the past year Yusuf had worked extremely hard to build a trustworthy relationship with Javier. When times were good, he would go to Cundinamarca and Javier would show VCR recordings of people hanging from trees with their bodies on fire, or dead corpses with guts hanging from the slice of machete, demonstrating what happened to those who double-crossed him.

Yusuf told Javier he didn't have $5 million dollars. So, he was taken to a steel cage located in the back of the camp next to the horse stables, with armed soldiers keeping watch over him. Yusuf wondered how long he would be kept alive.

Once a day, a soldier would allow Yusuf out of the cage to walk around in an area covered with dirt and the stench of manure. He knew that this was his only chance to escape.

Most nights Javier's men would have women over, entertaining them with Cumbia music and liquor late in the night. The women would dance until a couple of soldiers passed out from too much alcohol, often forgetting to lock Yusuf back in the cage. One night when the soldiers weren't paying attention Yusuf saw his moment. He grabbed a blanket to use as a cover and hightailed it to the wall. He threw the blanket around a pole that was sticking atop and looped it around so he could hold both ends. He then pulled himself up, scaling with his feet and flipped over the top to the ground on the other side.

He hustled down the rocky hillside terrain, tumbling and sliding without looking back, praying his captors hadn't realized he was gone as yet, so he could keep his head start. When he came upon a narrow road, he saw the headlights of an old gray Chevy truck with bales of hay in the bed and waved it down. The driver was an old Colombian man with white hair. Yusuf was trying to catch his breath. "Excuse m- me sir, c- could you give me a ride into town?"

"¿Que? Yo hablo un poco de ingles," The old man said.

"A ride to town."

"O, okay. Subete mi amigo."

Yusuf opened the passenger's-side door and quickly hopped in. "Thank you."

"¿Que haces en esta area?"

"I'm here on vacation. I was driving around and got lost. I saw a group of teenagers to ask for directions and they robbed me of my wallet and rental car."

"Lo siento, mi amigo."

Yusuf hoped he bought his story.

* * *

Yusuf's old associate Chico had been busted by the DEA and flipped into an informant.

Yusuf was unaware that Chico had provided information into his operation through Cuba. Agents knew that Yusuf used fishing vessels that went out far enough to rendezvous with speed boats that took kilos to the Florida Keys.

Once Yusuf returned to the U.S., one of his contacts in Miami told him what had taken place, and that he had been federally indicted. Yusuf knew he had to go somewhere and lay low, so he fled to Guadalajara, Mexico. There he rented a two-bedroom house in a secluded area on the edge of town.

In the mornings Yusuf would walk to a diner for breakfast and have bean burritos with eggs, jalapeños, fried fish and coffee. Some nights he would go to a bar to play pool and drink tequilas.

One night a young Mexican man asked him in broken English if he smoked marijuana.

Yusuf said he did, and the Mexican gave him a bud out of a small clear Ziploc baggy, along with rolling papers. They both went outside on the side of the bar and Yusuf rolled two cigarette joints. He lit one, put the other in his front pocket, and took a long drag before passing it to his new friend. They both stayed in the same spot until the joints were gone and they agreed to meet up again the following night.

The next morning Yusuf walked into the diner and ordered his usual breakfast, when he noticed two white men sitting at a table harassing a young petite Hispanic waitress. They were whistling and grabbing the bottom of her skirt every time she passed by to serve other customers. The waitress did her best to ignore them, who were obvious tourists.

One of them slapped the waitress on the buttocks and she turned around and spat a racial slur in Spanish that they took offence to. Both men quickly stood with their faces scrunched. Yusuf got up from his table and stepped in front of them. "Aye man, why don't ya'll just leave."

"Who in the hell are you to tell us to leave?" one of the men said. Yusuf could smell the sour stench of alcohol and morning breath.

"I'm just sayin', people are tryin' to eat and ya'll are being a disturbance."

"Go to hell!" The man shoved Yusuf in the chest knocking him backwards. The diner became silent as Yusuf regained his balance and lunged forward elbowing him square in the jaw. The man dropped to the floor unconscious. Yusuf then grabbed the second man by the neck in a headlock, and repeatedly punched him in the face until his eye split.

Yusuf had blood all over his shirt when the Mexican police arrived and all three were detained and taken to the local jail and placed in separate cells. The large holding cell smelled of aged funk and sweat. When Yusuf scanned over the dingy walls he noticed in the back corner, a hole in the floor for the toilet. There were two cells across from each other, with a narrow walkway straight down the center. Mexican inmates sat on the concrete with their backs aligned against the bars because there were no beds to lie on.

That first night Yusuf tried his best to stay awake because he didn't want to fall asleep surrounded by strange prisoners. But his eyes got heavy and he nodded off to sleep. When he awakened what seemed only a few minutes later, he realized his tennis shoes were gone; removed right off his feet. He stared at his socks in disbelief that he hadn't felt anything, then surveyed the cell but everyone appeared to be asleep. Contemplating if he should wake everyone by causing a scene, he decided against it, because he was the only American in the cell along with eight Mexicans.

The following morning for breakfast, jailhouse guards brought a tin pan to the cell piled with tamales. Everyone lined up and could get two apiece. Yusuf remained sitting until a young fit Mexican with short black hair asked him if he was hungry. Yusuf got up, went to the front to receive his portion of tamales, and handed them both to the fit Mexican who thanked him and said his name was Juan. Yusuf asked Juan if he knew English and he said yes, that he learned English from going to California to work at the farms. Yusuf told him what happened that night.

After the guards left Juan stood in the middle of the cell, spoke in Spanish, and one of the prisoners pointed to another. Juan then attacked the man who was implicated and discovered Yusuf's shoes tucked under the poncho in his pants.

Later that afternoon Yusuf saw a judge and was granted a bail. He posted the funds and was released. While walking alongside the only paved road in town, a red Jeep Wrangler with two male occupants pulled up next to him. "Hey partner, need a ride?" the driver asked, who was a middle-aged Hispanic.

"Um, yeah man. I do live a little ways from here."

"Well come on in, my name is Ramon." "And I'm Mike," the young Caucasian in the passenger seat said as he opened the door.

"My name is Yusuf; I appreciate the lift." Yusuf got in the rear seat.

Ramon looked at Yusuf in the rearview mirror. "Partner, where are you coming from?"

"Man, I just got out of jail for gettin' into a fight yesterday."

Mike turned in his seat to look back. "What happened?"

"Some stupid tourists were causin' a disturbance at the diner I ate at, and when I asked them to leave one of them put his hands on me."

"Did you kick their asses?" Mike smiled.

Yusuf flashed a grin. "I did my thang."

"Hey partner, you must be hungry."

"Yeah man, I'm starvin'."

Ramon drove until they spotted an eatery on the side of the road. He pulled the Jeep into the dirt lot, and they all got out and went in. There was a pool table located in the back. Mike put his hand on Yusuf's shoulder. "You want to shoot a couple rounds?"

Ramon went to the counter to buy three Corona's, took Yusuf and Mike one, and watched them play. When the second game was over, they all went to a table so they could sit and eat. Mike grabbed the menu from between the condiments holder and called the waitress over, who was a heavy-set Mexican lady wearing a hair net and white apron, and ordered everyone steak fajitas.

"So, Yusuf, you were saying that you were here on vacation earlier, when I was whoopin' your butt," Mike bragged with a smirk.

"Yeah man, I just needed to get away and relax from work."

"What kind of work do you do?"

"I buy and sell cars after I fix 'em up."

"Sounds pretty profitable."

"Yeah, I do okay for myself."

Something struck Yusuf as odd about the two men.

After they finished eating, Yusuf told them he was tired and needed to get home.

Ramon left a tip for the waitress, then they left and got back in the Jeep and drove down a dirt road that led to the front of Yusuf's house. He thanked Ramon and Mike for their generosity before getting out, and they turned around and drove into the late-noon dust.

When Yusuf walked through the front door, he kicked his shoes off, stripped to his boxers and tossed his clothes on the side of the couch. He then headed to the shower. When he got out, he went into the living room and sunk into the brown leather couch. He dug the remote from between the cushions and laughed to himself while he clicked through the channels. Finally, the tension subsided from his shoulders, at ease that he was no longer in a Mexican jail. His head fell back in drowsiness and he went to sleep.

It was sundown when a noise startled Yusuf. It sounded like something had fallen to the floor. Without realizing how long he had slept, Yusuf thought he heard whispers in the hallway. He got up to investigate, when in a sudden rush, four men appeared and grabbed him. They were wearing black tactical gear and yelling for him to get on the floor. Their weapons were pointed directly at his chest so he complied and was handcuffed. The men identified themselves as United States Marshals. When they stood him to his feet, he immediately recognized two of the men as Ramon and Mike.

Yusuf knew he had finally been caught when Ramon smiled and said, "Hi Trigga."

Only the L.A. Gang Task Force knew him by that name.

CHAPTER 4

Lee stayed in New Orleans with his grandmother until he completed high school, then moved back to California to attend Cal-Poly Pomona on a full academic scholarship. When he moved on campus to live in the dorms, he met his roommate Chris who was from Scottsdale, Arizona. Chris was six-foot-three, slender with fair skin and a crew cut. His father was a retired Wall Street broker from New York who moved his family to Arizona while Chris was still in elementary school.

Chris grew up privileged and almost didn't graduate high school because he would always get into fights, which constantly got him suspended. He chose to go to Cal-Poly because they offered him a Division II sports scholarship to wrestle.

Lee and Chris quickly became friends, even though their backgrounds were completely different. On the weekends they would go to the movies and afterwards, hang out and explore the entire city of Pomona.

At an early age Chris's father exposed him to the world of investing. His father also had an investment firm, so Chris knew certain things about the inner workings of Wall Street. One afternoon after class Lee noticed

Chris watching Bloomberg financial news and looking at a newspaper jotting down notes.

"Chris, what you doin'?"

"I'm looking at stock charts in Investor's Business Daily."

"Investor's Business…what?"

"It's a financial paper I use to research stocks."

"So, you own stocks?"

"Yeah bro, my father opened a Myrill Lynch brokerage account for me with $50,000 dollars, and also paid for me to attend an Investor's Business Daily Certification Program that starts this weekend downtown. So, I won't be able to hang out as much."

"That sounds interesting. What does the program teach you?"

"It's a curriculum that teaches fundamental and technical analysis bro. And everything is based on historical facts, not opinions, which allows you to achieve superior results from your trades."

"That sounds pretty intense."

"Bro, they also give lessons on chart reading and screening techniques directly from portfolio managers that teaches you when to hold winning stocks for bigger gains. This will give me the knowledge that I need instead of depending on my broker."

Lee wondered if it was possible for him to learn about the stock market and investing.

He had never met anyone who was in that world before, and for some odd reason it was attractive to him. "Can you make a lot of money investing in the stock market?"

"Bro, you can get rich."

It was clear to Lee that Chris's family was well off by the pictures he showed in his photo album of him and his family taking trips to Paris,

France standing under the Eiffel Tower. And of them posing in front of the pyramids in Giza, Egypt.

"Do you think I could learn that?"

"Anyone can learn. That's my father's philosophy anyway."

"How much does it cost to get in that program?"

"It costs around $10,000 dollars to complete the certification, and classes are Saturdays and Sundays from 9:00 a.m. to 5:00 p.m."

"Damn, that's a lot of money."

"If you're serious bro, I may be able to get my father to sponsor you. Then we could catch the bus downtown together and study during the week after class."

"Are you serious? Hell yeah, I'll learn it."

Chris talked with his father later that evening and convinced him to finance Lee's program. After their classes were done for the day, Chris would quiz Lee out of the investment books they checked out of the campus library.

"Bro, what are the four main indexes that gives a broad look at market?"

"The Dow Jones Industrial average tracks the 30 largest companies called the Blue Chips. The S&P 500 tracks 500 large cap companies, the Nasdaq Composite tracks companies that trade on the Nasdaq, and the NYSE composite tracks the companies that trade on the New York Stock Exchange."

"Why are the Dow Jones 30 companies called blue chips?"

"Because the most expensive chips in Vegas are the blue ones." Lee smirked, feeling like that was a trick question.

"Okay, what are the main trading places?"

"The New York Stock Exchange, the Nasdaq Exchange, and the American Exchange, which is called the Amex."

"How do you determine a large-cap, mid-cap, and small-cap company?"

"Cap means capitalization. A large-cap means the companies capitalization is worth $12 billion dollars or more. Mid-caps are worth $1 billion up to $12 billion, and small-caps are $500 million up to $1 billion. And to determine the cap size of a company, you multiply the share price by the number of shares outstanding."

"Alright bro, remember I told you that institutions such as mutual funds create 80 percent of the market movement?"

"Yeah, I remember."

"Not only that, most people are invested in them through their retirement accounts and have no idea how they work. The reason institutions like mutual funds, hedge funds, banks, and insurance companies move the markets like that is because they are accumulating millions and hundreds of thousands of shares at a time. So, what is a mutual fund?"

Lee Brushed down the waves on top of his head with his palm. "Um…a mutual fund is a basket of stocks that someone manages in a fund. There are different classes of funds that determines the management's investment style. Growth funds invest in companies that show the potential to grow from new innovative products. Value funds invest in older established companies whose stock is depressed relative to its book value. Income funds invest in companies that pay out quarterly dividends. Blended funds invest for income and value, and socially responsible funds invest in environmentally-friendly companies."

They would go at it for hours every evening, and their relationship grew. Lee shared his childhood of growing up in South Central, Los Angeles around gangs and poverty, and Chris shared his life of trips and exotic vacations.

At the end of their freshman year, they completed their certification program and Chris invited Lee to Arizona for summer break to meet his parents and to learn more at his fathers' firm, CP Financial. Lee took him up on his offer and was excited to go.

* * *

Lee and Chris disembarked Southwest Airlines 747, walked through the terminal to get their luggage from the baggage claim, and out through the doors of Sky Harbor Airport into the bright broiling sun of Phoenix, Arizona's mid-day summer. Chris's father Mr. Priest picked them up in a black Lincoln Navigator, and Chris opened the back trunk to put their bags in before the two got in with Lee getting in the rear seat.

"It's a pleasure to finally meet you, sir. I truly appreciate what you've done for me."

Mr. Priest glanced in the rearview mirror. "Your welcome Lee. I'm happy to have done it, and you'll learn a lot more."

"Man, it's like a smothering oven out there," Lee grumbled. Chris laughed. "You aint lyin' bro."

They arrived at Chris's house in Scottsdale, a luxurious home with a manmade pond on the west side of the house, and a tennis court on the east side. They went up the front entry walkway where a quintet of saguaro's was staged like steps and the lighting for the succulents were built into the roofline. They entered the solid glass front door which was embedded with iridescent chips that matched the interior's violet fuchsia accents. Once inside they walked across the oak barn wood gallery floor which spanned the front of the house. They went into the sunken front room where cast-in-place concrete walls with stacked stone, scored floors, and floor-to-ceiling windows combined to create a soothing aesthetic, led them into the kitchen where Chris's mother was baking cookies. "Hi, honey." Mrs. Priest gave Chris a hug.

"Hi mom, this is my friend Lee that I told you about."

"Oh, hi hon nice to finally meet you."

She opened her arms and Lee hugged Mrs. Priest. "It's my pleasure."

"I made cookies if you boys want any." Mrs. Priest took a sheet pan out of the oven, scooped the cookies with a spatula into a jar and placed the pan in the dishwasher. She kissed Chris on the cheek. "Honey I'm late for my yoga class, I'll see you boys later."

Mrs. Priest was a petite five-foot-three with sandy hair pulled back into a ponytail. Her eyes were an ocean blue that matched her T-shirt that was tied in a knot on the side. And the black spandex she wore showed off the curves of her butt and legs.

"Dear, I'll be at the office when you get back," Mr. Priest said.

"Okay." Mrs. Priest disappeared down the hallway.

"Chris, I'll be in the den for a little bit before I head to the office."

"Alright dad."

"Man, you have a nice house," Lee said.

"Come on bro, let me show you the guest room."

They went down a series of hallways to a bedroom door. Chris opened it, they went in and Lee looked around at the bronze-framed floral pictures of white orchids that hung on the sky-blue walls. In the middle of the room was a king size bed covered with a royal blue comforter, and against the wall a television stand with a 32-inch Sony Trinitron and a Nintendo.

"That's nice," Lee said.

"Let's go to my room, I want to show you something." They went directly across the hall to Chris's bedroom. Chris went to his desk where he had a McIntosh computer and removed a certificate from the top drawer.

"What is that?" Lee asked.

"A stock certificate bro."

"Why is Mickey Mouse and Donald Duck's picture on it?"

"This is a hundred shares of Disney. My father bought these shares as his first investment because my grandparents took him to Disneyland in the early '60s when he was a kid. He remembered how much fun he had and knew it would make money."

"Man, that's cool."

"Bro, follow me to the garage." They walked down a hallway where paintings of Vincent Van Gogh hung on the walls, to the den where Mr. Priest was sitting in a leather recliner smoking a cigar. Lee scanned the wall of photos of Mr. Priest holding golf clubs on different greens.

Mr. Priest noticed Lee's intrigue. "Have you ever been golfing?"

"No sir. But it looks like a lot of fun."

The stout man of six-foot-four got up from his chair, walked over to the wall and pointed to one of the pictures. "This golf course in Stanford, North Carolina is Tobacco road. The course was designed and crafted with the revolutionary eye of Mike Strants. It was originally a tract of North Carolina tobacco farmland that was later mined and excavated."

Lee pointed to a different photo. "What about this course?"

"That's Reynold's Lake Oconee in Greensboro, Georgia. That course is anchored by the Ritz-Carlton and tucked into the lake country between Atlanta and Augusta. I'll spend the days by the lake at Great Waters, which offer lake views on every hole. And that's also where I first tried out my Callaway Epic Star 50-gram shaft iron driver."

"Okay, okay dad, we have to go," Chris interrupted. "I want to show Lee around; we'll talk to you later."

Chris and Lee went through a side door that led to the garage, when a five-foot-five bronze-skinned Native female with long shiny black hair hanging down her back threaded into a braid, appeared out of nowhere. She weighed around 130 pounds and was dressed in an aqua blue skirt with a white short-sleeve blouse.

"Hello Chris, you're finally home," she said as she opened her arms.

"Sis, what's up?" They embraced each other. "This is my friend Lee from college. Bro, this is my sis Percilla."

Lee extended his hand. "Hi, nice to meet you."

"Nice to meet you too."

Captivated by Percilla's beauty, Lee seemed hypnotized. Her long eyelashes, pointed nose, and the thin lips between her dimples highlighted her cheekbones. She wore a Native nylon headband around her forehead with southwest designs. When she smiled her eyes twinkled.

"Alright sis, we'll be back later."

"Okay. It's good, your home."

Chris clicked on the lights where a grey Mercedes Benz, and a BMW 325i was parked. He grabbed a set of keys off the rack to the BMW and waved Lee over. "Bro, let's go for a drive."

The leather-wrapped black interior hugged Lee when he sat in the passenger's seat. He closed the door, rubbed the palm of his hand over the waves in his hair, and looked at Chris with his left eyebrow arched. "Your sister?"

"Bro, I know," Chris smiled. "You're wondering how she could be my sister. Our mothers were best friends, and both of her parents worked for my father as his accountants. They were in a fatal accident with a drunk driver when Percilla and I were in elementary school, so my parents made arrangements for her to live with us. Her family on the reservation was already overwhelmed with several kids."

"Oh, okay."

"So, she's like my sister because we pretty much grew up together. She spends a lot of time on her reservation and does a lot of community work for her Native tribe."

Chris opened the garage door, and slowly pressed his foot down on the pedal easing the car forward. Then with an extra tap of pressure, they zoomed out of the driveway.

CHAPTER 5

When Chris and Lee got back to the house Percilla was in the kitchen.

"It smells like you're makin' somethin' good sis."

"I was just making something before I left."

Lee was curious. "Where are you going?"

"To the Native American experience."

"What is the Native American experience?"

"It's a Native American platform that introduces guests to authentic Native culture and cuisine in a cocktail setting."

"It sounds interesting."

"Would you like to come?"

Surprised by the invitation Lee was thrown off guard. "Um…sure, I'll go."

"Yeah bro, go and have fun," Chris grinned.

"Would you like something to eat before we leave?" Percilla asked.

"Sure. I am pretty hungry," Lee said.

"Me too," Chris agreed.

"This may sound dumb, but since I've been here in Arizona, I always see those carved wooden structures of masks and eagles. I think they are called totem poles."

"Those are canoes, southwest spiritual posts. Europeans named them totem poles mistakenly assuming they were a feature of all Indian cultures."

"Oh, okay."

Percilla made cornflake-crusted fish-n-chips with whole-wheat breadcrumbs, parmesan cheese, cod fillets, and Greek yogurt mixed with relish, Dijon mustard, and black pepper for the tartar sauce. For the tots, she used 18-ounce sleeve polenta and diced them into bite sized pieces using virgin oil and black pepper. Once they were done, they all put their plates in the sink and washed up.

Percilla and Lee went to the garage, got into her red Honda Accord, and drove to the Scottsdale Amphitheater. When they arrived in the parking lot they got out of the car, went through the front to the large hall, and took a seat in the second row. It was brightly lit and smelled of sage mixed with different food aromas. An old Indian man with white hair walked on the stage to introduce the guests.

The American Indian Language Development Institute was honoring Daryl Baldwin from the Miami tribe of Oklahoma, and Marie Wilcox from the Wukchumni, along with Pima- Maricopa members for their years long work in preserving the Piipash language.

Lee was appreciating the experience of learning some things about Native American culture and was glad it was with Percilla. When the event ended everyone applauded with a standing ovation.

"Have you ever eaten Indian flat bread?" Percilla asked Lee.

"No, I haven't. Is it good?"

"Come on, let's go to the station over there." Percilla and Lee walked to a food table where a heavy-set middle-aged Indian woman gave them a flat bread apiece slathered with honey and powdered sugar.

"This is good," Lee said.

"I know, I love to eat it freshly-made."

When they finished tasting different foods at the food stations, they went back outside through the exits. "That was pretty enlightening to know there are people around keeping your Native language alive."

"Our cultural language has to be preserved or it will be lost. So I contribute to the cause by being in the 'Uuduushik.'"

"What does that mean?"

"It means, 'we are the people.'"

"How long have you been learning the language?"

"About four years now, and there are only about a dozen fluent speakers of Piipash left in Arizona."

"That's a great thing to do, because I am of African descent and not only has our language been lost, but our names were taken away as well." They got into Percilla's car and left the theater.

When they returned home, Percilla led Lee to her bedroom. "I want to show you something, if that's alright."

"Okay, that's fine."

In her room were two large dressers made of cherry wood with bronze handles next to a queen sized bed covered with a handmade woven blanket that bore Southwest Indian designs.

On her wall hung Native paintings in silver frames of a ritual cere-mony of Mandan O-Kee-Pa, and Old Bear, a Mandan medicine man in 1832. Directly hanging over her headboard was a life-like painting of the Plains warrior, Sioux Chief Sitting Bull.

Percilla sat on her bed, slid open her top drawer, and took out what looked like a brown diary book with a raised imprint of a buffalo on the cover. She patted the mattress next to her. "Sit down."

"What is that?" Lee asked.

Percilla took a folded piece of paper out of the book, opened it and began reading:

"You see, I am alive

You see, I stand in good relation to the earth

You see, I stand in good relation to the Gods

You see, I stand in good relation to all that is beautiful

You see, I stand in good relation to you

You see, I am alive, I am alive."

Lee took a few seconds to absorb its meaning. "Who wrote that?"

"No one knows. But it is a Plains Indian prayer that I recite every morning after I wake up."

Lee could see Percilla was a very spiritual person.

"Do you believe in heaven and hell?" he asked.

"I believe we go to a spirit world after this life. What about you?"

"I don't know if I believe in an afterlife. I've seen a lot of death growing up, how could anyone know?"

"Because the desire for eternal life is something fundamental to us. It's embedded in our essential nature."

"What do you mean by that?"

"Well Lee, as soon as we gain some relief from the turmoil of this material life and have the opportunity to reflect and turn inwards, we begin to think of life after death and feel empty. Because we realize this world is not permanent."

"But how does that indicate we go somewhere after this?"

"Well, there are many people who deny belief in an afterlife, but at the same time they strive to leave a good name behind before they die. Why would someone who regards death as the end of all things be concerned for their good reputation or for acts of charity that outlive them? There would be no point in expending such an effort for something that has no reality.

Once life comes to an end, how could an achievement, or even an evil act to be remembered, benefit someone who denies life after death?"

Lee allowed the question to sink in. "I don't know."

"I believe it's because such a person is acting, in reality, according to the desire of their innermost being; they are demonstrating that in fact they do believe in their own immortality."

For a brief moment Lee reflected on his mother and father, family and friends, and wondered if he would see them again in the spirit world. He looked at Percilla and locked eyes, then leaned in to kiss her. Lee brought his lips to meet Percilla's with a soft touch, slowly easing his tongue into her mouth to find hers; twirling and gliding like a sweet dance. Her lips were soft and smooth, and he sucked them like a bitten strawberry. Lee pulled the blouse from the waist of her skirt and unbuttoned it to reveal her bra. He gently laid the back of her head on the pillow, simultaneously picking her legs up to place them on the bed.

Lee leveraged himself on his forearms hovering over Percilla as they passionately tongued one another. She began untucking his shirt, so he raised onto his knees, pulled it over his head, and gazed into her eyes. *She was the depiction of Pocahontas,* he thought. Lee tossed his shirt on the floor and began kissing her chin, voyaging down the curve of her neck as she turned her head slightly to the right. Her gasps of air every time he sucked her skin, aroused him to impatience. But there was no way he would hurry, he wanted to savor every moment with her.

Lee reached behind Percilla and she arched her back so he could unfasten her bra.

Sliding the straps down her shoulders, he dropped it on the side of the bed. Percilla's breasts were firm and her nipples perked, growing harder from him gliding the tip of his tongue around and under the side by her armpit. Lee enjoyed the taste of her skin, it felt like silk against his tongue as it circled around her areola with Percilla quivering to its touch.

In a moment of clarity, Lee realized they hardly knew one another, and he wanted this to be a memory of a lifetime. He could barely believe how gorgeous Percilla was as he put her right nipple between his lips, sucking and glistening it with saliva. Lee rotated between both breasts while Percilla moaned and slithered beneath him. The tip of his tongue made it to the middle of her chest then trailed to her belly button. Her stomach was flat and smooth, and he continued licking and kissing until he reached the fabric of her skirt. Lee slid it down her waist and dropped it next to the slip-on sandals she was wearing. Then kissed up the inside of her thigh until he reached her panties and inhaled the fresh scent of her juices. Lee slid the side of the lace down Percilla's legs, and around her ankles, then removed his own pants along with his boxers. For a brief moment, he just stared at Percilla's body like a piece of art.

Percilla's trust spoke to Lee when she opened her legs while he licked the inside of her thigh. The area was soft and tender. He put her legs down to position himself on the left side of her and grabbed under her left leg to bend her knee across the bottom of his stomach to spread her. With Lee's right arm cradling the back of Percilla's head as she faced him, he kissed the tip of her nose. And with his left, Lee used the flats of his fingers to lightly tease and stroke around her vulva and labia, coating his fingers. He then explored above the clitoris where the shaft extends, gently tickling it in a circular motion.

Percilla's moans and winces drove Lee crazy every time she exhaled her sweet breath against his face. And he could feel the first of a series of shakes knowing she was cuming, by the amount of cream between his fingers. Lee could feel how swollen Percilla's clit had gotten as he continued rubbing it to stimulate blood flow. He positioned himself over the top of her and pushed her legs apart with his thighs, ready to enter her. Lee slid his right forearm under the back of Percilla's neck, held his penis with his left hand, and parted her moist lips with the head. She flinched. Lee slowly pushed his hips forward, released his penis, and reached behind her to grip under her torso so he could enter her completely.

Percilla wrapped her arms tightly around Lee's back and locked her heels over his calves with a grip that made them one. The deep thrusts caused her to squeal into his ear. The side of Percilla's face pressed against his, and Lee held her like a delicate flower. Feeling the tightness, he slid in and out of her slowly and cautiously knowing he had to be gentle. Every time Lee pushed deep within Percilla he could feel his testicles against the crack of her butt where the juices trailed. Their bodies moved in harmony like a symphony to create beautiful music and Lee was the conductor; Percilla's shakes and shivers the orchestra.

CHAPTER 6

She was standing in line at the concession stand in the stadium holding a cup of beer in her right hand, and a red snap Gucci bag in the other, when a couple of quarters slipped through her fingers. Their eyes locked when they simultaneously bent down. "Oh, let me help you with that." Lee picked the change off the floor and handed it to her.

"Thank you so much."

The fair-skinned woman with sandy blond shoulder-length hair and hazel eyes was balancing a cup of beer, trying to put the money in her handbag.

"Let me hold that for you." Lee reached for her drink and she handed it to him.

"I appreciate it, thanks. I'm so clumsy sometimes."

"You're welcome. It's no problem," Lee said.

The lady left and Lee was next in line. He ordered a chili-cheese hot dog, Coke, and beer, which the young man behind the counter placed in a cup holder. Then he headed back to the stands for kick-off. While walking through the isle of seats to his section squeezing through people excusing himself, he saw the woman he'd just helped sitting in the row directly behind Jahi.

"Well, hello again."

Lee gave the chili-dog and Coke to Jahi.

"Hi," she responded. Her smile displayed perfectly white teeth. She was sitting next to a young man who nodded.

"So we meet again," Lee said.

"Since I didn't get a chance to introduce myself, my name is Nicole. And this is my brother Dave."

"Nice to meet you Nicole and Dave. I'm Lee, and this is my nephew Jahi."

"Hello," Jahi said. They all shook hands

Lee and Jahi drove up to Palo Alto from L.A. the day before in order to find a good suite knowing there would be a lot of bookings in the area. The University of Southern California was playing Stanford University, and it would had been hard to find a room had they arrived the day of the football game.

"This should be a pretty good game don't you think?" Nicole said.

"Maybe. But I hope you don't take this loss personal," Lee smirked. He could see she and Dave were Stanford fans by the colors they wore.

"We'll just see if those cocky USC players will be eating humble pie today," Nicole grinned.

After about an hour it was halftime and Stanford led 17-14. Lee looked back and asked Nicole and Dave if they wanted anything before the second half. Dave politely declined and Nicole went with Lee.

"So, where are you from," Lee asked.

"I'm from right here in the Bay area, San Francisco. What about you?"

"I'm from L.A."

"I should have known by your USC cap."

"So, are you a 49ers fan?"

"You better believe it," Nicole stated proudly.

"Well, that's one thing we definitely have in common. Even though I'm from Los Angeles, the 9ers are my squad." They both chuckled.

It was their turn to be served and Lee bought two beers and gave Nicole one. She thanked him and they headed back to their seats where Jahi and Dave was talking.

"Jahi, are you in school?" Nicole asked.

"Yes, I'm in graduate school with my Bachelor's in finance."

"Oh, that's excellent."

"I only have a year left to get my MBA."

"That's impressive. I wish the best for you."

"Thank you."

"Nicole, what about you. What do you do?" Lee asked.

"I work as a fund manager for Myrill Lynch in the San Francisco financial district."

"Really. You have to be kidding. Well that's another thing we have in common, because right as we speak, I'm waiting on SEC approval to start my own hedge fund investment firm."

"Wow, that's amazing. What made you want to start your own company?"

"Back when I was in college I was mentored by a good friend of mine. His father has a financial firm in Arizona where I interned. I eventually started working for him as a broker for about six years after I graduated. I learned a lot about the business, but I got homesick so I went back to L.A. and worked as an executive equity analyst at Vanguard for another eight years. Then I took some time off and traveled to Africa and Asia for a few years."

"That sounds special."

"Thanks. So when I returned, I finally decided to start my own firm."

They enjoyed the remainder of the football game. USC 24, Stanford Cardinals 20, was the final score when they all stood with the crowd to leave the stadium.

"Only one more game to win and we're in the Pac 10 Championship game," Jahi clapped and smiled while they exited through the tunnel. Lee looked at Nicole and flashed a grin when they entered the parking lot.

"Can I see your phone so I can dial in my number?" Nicole said.

"Okay." Lee took his phone out of his front pocket and handed it to her.

"Call me."

"I sure will. You two be safe."

They said their good-byes and went in different directions to their cars.

* * *

Lee gave his car keys to the valet, and he and Jahi walked through the lobby of the Hilton Resort in Beverly Hills to attend a private event where Nicole was giving a seminar. She was considered to be one of the industry's leading financial analysts, and Lee wanted Jahi to listen to her economic overview.

It had been almost two years since the launch of CYGNUS Investments, and Lee and Nicole had developed a close relationship. Nicole had referred several associates to Lee's firm, who followed her blogs and weekly webinars on MonsterTrader.com where she gave market analyses and educational commentary.

Nicole graced her thin five-foot-seven frame across the stage wearing a long black Nehera leather jacket with a white turtleneck sweater, and black slacks with black low-heel dress shoes. Her bob-style cut revealed diamond studded earrings. She looked every bit the professor waving to the spectators, peering behind the lenses of her black framed Tom Ford's with her wide smile. The audience's applauses echoed through the assembly room that sat over three hundred guests as they stood to give a warm welcome.

"Ladies and gentlemen, when you see an index such as the S&P 500 going up and up it may look good on a chart, and the technical indicators may even look excellent at a glance, but you have to ask yourself if it is a realistic reflection of strong economic growth," she began. "Is there anything beneath the surface that we may not be seeing? If you are into the fundamentals, then you'll be keeping an eye on such things as the unemployment rate, GDP growth, and growth in the manufacturing sector, as a few examples. What is the general trend? Is it also growing, or is it slowing down? Or are you seeing signs of a divergence where one or more of the sectors are going up, while others are slowing down or heading down? I'm not saying that any of these factors will give you a clear guide as to what to expect going forward, but the idea is that you should be looking for signs of any anomalies that could indicate a change in sentiment. And if you see signs that suggest a change in the direction of the markets, then pull up your charts and bring up indicators that have to do with market internals such as breadth and sentiment, and see if they're still growing strong because the S&P 500 may be continuing on its extended bull run with strong signs of complacency. All indicators may be suggesting a continuation of the current trend, overall sentiment is bullish, and you may have enough time to be the next YouTube sensation."

The audience laughed.

"But the reality is that you may wake up one morning to the news of some geopolitical event that shook the markets. The markets in Asia and Europe may have slid down more than 3 percent, and the S&P futures market following its lead. So, when the markets open they could already be down more than 2 percent. That 2 percent may not sound like much, but it is enough to put the markets into a panic mode and send it spiraling down."

Nicole gave financial gems for nearly two hours before concluding, and the crowd gave a standing ovation as she waved good-bye. Lee and Jahi went to the dressing room area and stood in the hallway to wait for her. When Nicole came out, she spotted them and walked in their direction.

"Hey," Lee smiled.

"Hi." Nicole embraced him with a tight squeeze.

"That was a great lecture."

"Thank you."

"You remember my nephew Jahi, don't you?"

She leaned in to give him a hug. "Of course, how are you Jahi?"

"I'm fine. I really enjoyed the seminar."

"Thanks. I hope you got something from it."

"We should go for a drink," Lee insisted.

"Sure, why not. God knows I could use one," Nicole said.

They all went to the parking lot and Lee gave the valet his ticket, who returned in a silver S-Class Mercedes Benz. They got in with Jahi getting in the back seat, and Nicole suggested they go to a country and western bar on Beverly Hills Boulevard.

The night was still young when they arrived, and they trickled in with the customers through the front door where contemporary country music blared from the jukebox. Lee noticed Jahi bobbing his head. "Nephew what do you know about that?"

"Unc, that's Kelsea Ballerini."

Lee slowly shook his head and grinned as they walked to the counter. "What do you two want to drink?"

"I'll have whatever you're having," Nicole said. "And I'll have a Hennessey and Coke."

"Two raspberry Ciroc's, and a Hennessy and Coke please," Lee told the bartender. When they received their drinks, Nicole took a sip. "This is pretty good."

Lee took a swallow of Ciroc. "Nicole, there is something I would like to ask you."

"Okay, what's that?"

"I have a position at the firm that I need filled with someone I can trust. And I was wondering if you would consider being CYGNUS Investments' Chief Investment Officer?"

Nicole was silent for a few seconds, then took another drink. I'm honored you thought of me, but that's something I'll have to think about."

"That's fine, take as much time as you need."

As the three talked, Jahi knew he would be the designated driver by default. So, after his one drink he ordered lemon water and asked Nicole investment questions. When they were ready to leave Lee got his wallet, took out a $100 dollar bill and covered it with his empty glass, then gave Jahi his car keys.

"Jahi, could you take me back to the resort?" Nicole asked as they walked out the door.

"Sure, no problem."

It was late night and the California breeze whispered through the city when…pop, pop, pop, pop…the deafening cracks from a barrage of bullets rang out penetrating the silence. Lee instinctively covered Nicole and Jahi. Suddenly, he felt a burning sensation in the back of his leg. It buckled and he fell.

Nicole dropped her purse. "Oh my God! Lee!" she yelled.

"Unc!" Jahi shouted. He picked Lee up by the arm so they could find cover and he hobbled with Jahi and Nicole behind a parked car. People ran in all directions screaming as more shots were fired.

The gunman was a clean-shaven middle-aged man with a short buzz cut, who wore blue jeans and a white T-shirt. He walked down the sidewalk like he hadn't done anything, stood in front of a closed clothing store and waited.

Soon police sirens blared as they approached the scene and surrounded the suspect. The officers demanded he drop his weapon. Instead, the gunman began firing at police. Through a hail of bullets that lasted less than 30 seconds, the man lay dead on the curb. It was suicide by cop.

The perpetrator was a Marine Veteran who had just returned from a tour in Afghanistan and suspected his wife of ten years of having an affair. He followed her in a rental car to the bar Lee, Nicole, and Jahi were at, and watched her through the window kiss another man. So he went in unnoticed and pulled a Glock .45 automatic out of the small of his back, approached the unsuspecting lover, and shot him in the forehead. With his wife in shock begging for her life, she attempted to run. The husband trailed behind her. As soon as she reached the sidewalk, he unloaded four bullets into her back as her body slumped to the pavement. One of the bullets went through her side and ricocheted off the sidewalk hitting Lee in the back of his thigh. The husband stood over his wife with her body between his legs and delivered three more shots to the back of her head.

Ambulances screamed to the scene, and EMT first responders arrived in time to strap Lee onto a gurney and rush him to the hospital.

CHAPTER 7

Lee was released from the hospital after three days, with his leg bandaged. After two weeks on bed rest, he decided to go back to the office for a meeting to discuss new changes for CYGNUS Investments.

All of CYGNUS' board members were sitting in their chairs organizing notes and preparing paperwork when Lee spotted Ashtiyani through the window. She strutted in her black pants suit, and her straight black shoulder-length hair shone from the overhead lights when she entered the boardroom. Ashtiyani laid her briefcase on the table and unfastened the clasps.

Her bronze skin highlighted the gold Movado watch she wore. "Good morning guys, sorry I'm a little late."

Ashtiyani went to the coffee pot that was sitting on a round wooden table in the corner of the room. She poured herself a cup while everyone looked. She then took a seat at the table and sipped through the steam as she took documents out of her briefcase.

Ashtiyani pushed her square wire-framed Armani's up the bridge of her nose and noticed an unfamiliar face at the table. Who was this person she wondered?

"Okay, did everyone receive notice of waver?" Lee asked.

"Yes," all the board members said simultaneously.

Lee sat a recorder in the middle of the oval table.

"The Meeting of CYGNUS Investments, a California Limited Liability Company is held on this second day of February 2018. Present are all Members as follows: Chief Executive Officer Lee Prince, Executive Investment Analyst Jahi Davis, Chief Investment Officer Nicole Fitzpatrick."

Ashtiyani shot Lee a look.

"And Ashtiyani Salman Chairwoman and Executive Officer. Managers are: Lisa Johnson and Glenn Cephus, hedge fund analysts. Today, I want to discuss how CYGNUS Investments needs to employ different options contracts strategies not only on stocks, but also commodities and real estate. This will enable our team to increase CYGNUS Investments' asset valuation from the current $3 billion to $7 billion over the next 36 months, as we continue to grow our client base. I'll now defer to Nicole, our new Chief Investment Officer, who will elaborate in detail."

Nicole removed a stack of prospectuses from her briefcase and handed them all one.

"May I please direct your attention to page two, section one. As you can see experienced traders always look for ways to improve the risk-reward characteristics of a position by looking for the greatest possible margin for error. This philosophy is no less to directional strategies, as in volatility strategies. In directional strategies, as in volatility strategies, this can often be done by finding an appropriate spread. The vertical spread always consists of one long, purchased option and one short, sold option, where both the options are of the same type, either both calls or both puts, and their expiration dates are the same. Please turn to page three, section one. The example that's shown is, we purchase one September 50 call contract, and sell one September 55 call contract. As you can see, we have a five-dollar spread, which is our risk exposure. Or, if we purchase one June 45 put contract, and sell one June 40 put contract, we would still have the five-dollar spread exposure on the bearish side. Essentially, we use funds collected from the premiums of the contracts we sell to help pay for the contracts we purchase. Furthermore, the price of the contract is always an important consideration in making trading decisions. In order to trade intelligently, we need to know value as well as price. And as we know, the value of an option is determined by the volatility of the under-lying contract over the life of the option."

For nearly an hour, Nicole covered a range of trading techniques that would increase returns, before concluding.

"Thank you Nicole," Lee said. "There, being no further business to come before the meeting, upon motion duly made, seconded, and unan-imously carried, this meeting is adjourned." Everyone got up from their chairs and began exiting the room.

"Ashtiyani, hold up a second. Would you join me for brunch?"

Lee could see she was irritated by how quickly she looked back at him over her shoulder.

"You didn't think to tell me you were bringing on a new C.I.O.?"

"I didn't think I had to explain to anyone who I brought in to help the firm."

"I'm just sayin', you could've at least given me a heads up."

"You know what, you're right. I should have had the courtesy to let you know. It just happened to be the right opportunity at the right time, and I had to take advantage once it presented itself. Now, will you please join me?"

Ashtiyani let out a light exhale. "Sure, where would you like to go?"

"I know this really delicious Hawaiian spot."

They walked to the elevators and Lee pressed the down-arrow button. When the bell rung, the door opened and they went to the first floor. At the lobby, they went through the rotating doors and into the parking lot. "Let's take my car." Ashtiyani unzipped her blue leather Balenciago triangle handbag and took out her keys.

They went to a sleek mango colored BMW 8 Series. The design, with its distinctive twin- kidney grille, stretched out vertical bars, four-lens headlamps that were flattened faceted and angled on the upper edges, gave an unforgettable impression. She turned off the alarm and unlocked the doors.

"I see you have a taste for powerful cars," Lee joked.

"I guess you could say that, I just got it a few days ago."

The vehicle displayed an elegant exterior with materials and finishes Lee admired, once he opened the door. There were at least nine strong horizontal lines across the tail, which had a large black section encompassing giant exhaust ports with a screen air outlet port between them. Lee noticed below the grille resided four distinctive panels, all textured with the upper three framed by painted panels with the lowest opening entirely within a black section underlying the entire nose. When he sat in the leather seat it felt as though he were sitting in a space ship.

Lee closed the door. "This is nice."

"Thanks." Ashtiyani pressed the start button and pushed her foot down on the gas pedal, revving the 523-horse powered engine like they were at a start line. The 4.4-liter twin- turbo V-8 roared as she played with the infotainment system before backing out of the parking space. She touched the panel screen, turned on the stereo, and the crispness of a live Kenny G concert vibrated through the speakers, then drove out of the lot into traffic.

Once they got on the freeway, Lee gave Ashtiyani directions toward North Hollywood. They pulled into the parking lot of Pokéworks, a little Hawaiian fish place, got out of the car, and went in the front entrance.

"This is one of my favorite places," Lee said.

Ashtiyani read the name on the front window. "Poke?" she mispronounced.

"No, it's pronounced 'Pokay,'" Lee corrected as they went through the door. Instantly, they smelled the aroma of fresh fish, gourmet sauces, and spices.

Ashtiyani opened her nostrils and deeply inhaled. "It smells so good in here."

"I know hunh. Poké is a classic street food of chopped fish tossed with sea salt, seaweed and kukui nuts."

"I want the salmon bowl."

"Okay. And I'll get the lemon shark."

Lee ordered their bowls along with two Hawaiian Kona Lagers. Once they were seated Ashtiyani dug her fork in the bowl and scooped a nice portion into her mouth. "Mmm, this is pretty good."

"I told you, I try to eat here as often as I can. They also have excellent red snapper, blue marlin, and octopus bowls." Ashtiyani closed her eyes when she took another mouthful, and Lee could tell she had fallen in love with Poké.

"This salmon is so fresh."

"I'm glad you like it. I asked you to lunch to tell you I'll be going to Puerto Rico for a couple of days to handle some possible business opportunities for CYGNUS, and I need you to coordinate with Nicole while I'm gone."

Ashtiyani was quiet for several seconds before answering. "Alright," she mumbled.

Lee knew Ashtiyani was special ever since they first met three years prior at the Traders Expo in Las Vegas. He had total trust and confidence in her. She was a major contributor to the successful launch of CYGNUS Investments.

"Do you have any plans today? Because you can take the rest of the day off if you'd like. I can just have Nicole and Jahi take care of everything for today." Lee took a bite of Poké and a swallow of beer.

"Well, the Fakka Foundation is holding a fundraiser later, so I'll attend that."

"Fakka. What does that mean?"

"It means, to free a slave or prisoner."

"Oh, so what does the foundation do?"

"It's a humanitarian organization that raises money to buy medical supplies to send to torn areas of Palestine."

"I've never heard of it."

"It was established by a group of Palestinian-American women who follow the ideals of

Leila Khaled."

"Who is Leila Khaled?"

"Leila was a trained hijacker who orchestrated the taking of a TWA Boeing 707 in 1969." "What? How did she manage to do that?"

"She boarded a plane headed to Rome. Once the plane landed, she spent two days just walking the streets contemplating her mission. Then in the early hours of the morning of August 29th, Leila caught a bus to Fiumicino Airport on the outskirts of Rome, meeting with her associate who she only saw in a photo as they exchanged pre-arranged hand signals. His name was Salim Issawi, a Palestinian from Haifa. The two then boarded the Boeing 707 that was going to Athens, Greece. Once they were on the plane a flight attendant asked if the two wanted anything to eat, or if they needed pillows and blankets, to which Leila took one. She placed the blanket over her lap, took a hand grenade out of her purse, and put her pistol right on top of her trousers."

"Are you serious, then what?"

"Well, she then gestured Salim toward the cockpit right at the moment a hostess was opening the door with the crew's lunch trays. Salim seized the opportunity and leapt in front of the hostess causing her to scream. Leila rushed behind Salim and ordered the stewardess out of the way and Salim barked to the crew that the plane had been taken over."

"Damn, so where did they go?"

"They went to Syria, where they landed and handed over their weapons to authorities, and all the hostages."

"What were they trying to accomplish by high jacking a plane?"

"They took the plane because it was an American plane and they blamed America for helping Israel in their efforts to control Palestinian land."

"So, what happened to the hostages?"

"They were later released."

"What about Leila Khaled and her partner?"

"They fled, and Leila attempted a second hijacking after undergoing cosmetic surgery to change her looks."

"What, you gotta be jokin.'"

"No, I'm serious. And she always wore on her ring finger, a grenade pin wrapped around a bullet, as a symbol of being married to the struggle. That's why I wear this grenade pin on my necklace. She flamboyantly overcame the patriarchal restrictions of Arab society where women are traditionally subservient. Leila became an icon."

"Man, what a way to make a statement."

Lee and Ashtiyani finished eating and were ready to leave. They got up from the table, threw their empty bowls and cups in the trash, and left the establishment.

CHAPTER 8

It was 1:00 p.m. when Lee's plane landed in the capital city of San Juan, Puerto Rico. The air was thick with humidity when he walked out the sliding doors of the airport to meet his business partner Eduardo, who was a real estate developer.

Eduardo was a pudgy, brown-skinned five-foot-six, who had a short curly top that was faded to the skin on the sides. He grew up near the capital but moved to New York with relatives to attend college where he graduated from NYU with a master's degree in economics.

"¿Como estas?" Lee said, as he bro-hugged Eduardo who met him in the lounge.

"Todo bien mi amigo." Eduardo was excited Lee finally made it. Accompanying Eduardo was a tall caramel-skinned Hispanic woman. "Lee, this is my assistant Jessica who will be helping us find the best property locations."

"Well, hello." Lee gently took her hand.

"Nice to meet you Mr. Prince, I've heard a lot about you," Jessica said in broken English.

Jessica wore a grey and blue Alexander Wang mini-dress with a low-cut neckline, and black strap open-toe heels that highlighted her calves. The charcoal shine of her hair twirling down her shoulders looked off a Sasoon commercial as she stood five-foot eleven in front of Lee.

"Lee…Lee," Eduardo called.

Lee snapped out of his daze. "Oh, I'm sorry, what were you saying?"

"We will be looking at areas that will be hard to reach because of debris that's still around from hurricane Maria. Even though it's been over a year, there are still flattened houses that made hundreds of thousands of people homeless. And the people who do have shelter, many of them live under tarp roofs," Eduardo explained.

The three walked to Eduardo's black Chevy Silverado in the parking lot. They began driving through the city and Lee noticed destroyed homes on every street. "How would real estate options work on the island?" Lee asked.

"The real estate options are to gain control of a parcel of property without actually buying it. Such as a purchase option, which gives us the right to buy land at a predetermined price. And since we'll have full control, we'll have equitable interest. We can structure a contractual agreement where we can take control of 80 lots worth $3 million dollars of land using a purchase option for only $10,000 dollars."

"So how would we limit our exposure to risk?"

"It is important that we don't take title to the property because that affects the assessed value. Once title transfers, we become responsible for the taxes and liability, which we don't want. The beauty of this is that we can take control, in the sense of having the right to buy and resell the property. All we do is pay the premium for the option contract which is the $10,000 dollars; a fraction of the property. This is a wasting asset, so if we don't exercise our option contract, meaning use our right to buy the land, then we lose our entire premium or $10,000."

"Okay, what about a lease-purchase option strategy after we build the structures on the lots?"

"CYGNUS Investments could agree to lease a piece of real estate to someone who agrees to pay the lease with the option of buying it on, or before, the end of the lease-purchase option. This technique is perfect for low-end housing developments on our lots because leasers are generally attracted to lease-purchase options to get houses. They don't have the down payments to obtain conventional loans.

So we would offer lease-purchase options and structure it in such a way that we'll make a higher return than renting or selling the property. And there is a larger universe of buyer- leasers-renters than of those who can afford a home, and the idea of living in a home rather than an apartment is appealing in itself."

Lee turned to Jessica. "What do you think?"

"I think it's very advantageous because you'll attract a leaser by offering what appears at first to be a lease payment that is slightly higher than the average going rent, but with a portion of each month's rent going into an account. Then the funds in the account are available for a down payment when the leaser is ready to buy a home."

"Exactly," Eduardo said. "So CYGNUS Investments would write up the terms stating that if the leasee does not buy the property at the end of the lease, they forfeit the amount in the home equity account."

"Okay, when I return to L.A. I'll go over this with my C.I.O. Nicole and see what she thinks."

"Good, Jessica booked the both of you a flight into New York that leaves tonight. And you can get a connecting flight to LAX."

For the rest of the afternoon they continued to drive around looking at vacant lots for property locations.

* * *

Lee and Jessica arrived at La Guardia Airport a little after 11:00 p.m. They went through the terminal to the baggage claim, picked up their luggage, and left the lounge to find a taxi to take them to Manhattan.

The cab pulled in front of Jessica's building where she lived in a condominium on the 14th floor. Lee got their bags from the trunk and they entered the building to the elevators. When they got to Jessica's floor and went to the door, she typed a security code on her iPhone that turned off the alarm. "Make yourself at home, you can sit the bags on the side of the wall," she said.

Lee sat the luggage next to the coat rack then took a seat on a white curved Vladimir Kagan couch in the living room, which smelled of fresh sandalwood. "It smells nice in here."

"Thank you. Would you like a cup of coffee?" Jessica sat her purse and phone on a glass table next to the couch before she went to the kitchen.

"Yes, I would."

"Cream or sugar?"

"It doesn't matter."

Lee looked around the room and admired the beautiful décor. Placed neatly in Jessica's living room were pieces of Sumerian sculptures, and the area was decorated with a Danish Jorgen Hanson credenza next to a green '40s lounge chair. He got up to walk around.

"You don't mind me browsing around do you?"

"Of course not."

Lee went down the west hallway and saw a meditation room with pictures on the walls of Arabian paintings in Arabic script. Next to the window was a purple wave-shaped '70s sofa by Italian designer Giovanni Offredi. Lee casually continued to look through the rooms and noticed that arranged over every available surface in the loosely defined space were pre- Columbian figures, tiny bronze Buddhas, and Japanese lacquer boxes with silk cords.

"This is some place you have here," Lee said from the hallway.

"Thank you. I put a hint of cinnamon in your coffee, I hope you don't mind."

"No, that's fine."

Lee went through the sliding door to the terrace that overlooked the Hudson River and much of Downtown Manhattan. On the lip of the terrace were planted arrangements of Scotch pine, and Japanese grasses that created a wilderness affect. When he walked back to the front room, there was a white and black marble chess board on one of the glass tables against the wall. Jessica came into the living room with two mugs and handed one to Lee. "Be careful, it's hot."

They sat on the couch next to each other.

"Do you play chess? I see you have a really nice board," Lee said.

"No, not really, it's pretty much there for decoration. A girlfriend of mine gave it to me for my birthday."

"When is your birthday?" Lee blew through the steam of coffee and took a sip.

"Actually, it's coming up in a few weeks. Alexa, play Jessica's play list."

Sade's "No ordinary love" whispered through the surround sound speakers of her entertainment system.

Jessica scooted next to Lee, sat her cup on the table, then turned and softly kissed him on the cheek. Lee put his coffee down and Jessica took his hand to follow her to the bedroom. When they got to the bed Jessica faced him and the tips of their noses touched. Lee pulled her by the hips, lowered his mouth, and pressed his lips against hers. She gasped when he slid his tongue into her mouth. Gently and deeply he drew her in.

Lee pressed against Jessica so she could feel the huge bulge between his legs, and she reached behind him to untuck the shirt from his pants. He slid his hands up the back of her thighs under the black skirt she wore and cupped the mound of her butt. Jessica slid her skirt down, wiggled out of it, and unbuttoned her blouse to reveal the white matching Victoria's Secret bra and lace panties.

"Nice," Lee said.

"You like?" she whispered.

Lee took off his shirt, loosened his belt, and lowered his pants to step out of the legs. Jessica unhooked the back of her bra and exposed her 36 C's. He kissed the caramel skin of her neck and inhaled the sweet scent of Dior.

Jessica laid on the bed and Lee crawled over on top of her. He scooped his arms behind her back and lifted her to pull the comforter from beneath them. The satin sheets were cool, and the expanse of his broad chest felt the warmth of her breast pressed against him as he leaned down to taste her lips again. Jessica touched to know him, the smooth feel of his back as she caressed him, the tension of each muscle that shifted when he moved. Lee made her neck tingle with the touch of his moist lips, then tongued her nipples to make them his. "You taste so good," he whispered.

"Ohh," she moaned. Jessica was smooth as silk, every plane and curve of her body was firm, and Lee's mouth found exquisite ways to make her flesh submit. He leaned on the right side of her, reached down to remove her panties, and pulled them down her thighs. He took off his own briefs and got back on top of her. Jessica opened her legs to welcome the sting of

Lee's first penetration. She gave a small whimper. Then absorbed the thrust of the second with a sigh of pleasure..."unnhh."

CHAPTER 9

It was nightfall when the cruise liner left California's Southwest Coast from Catalina Island to set sail towards the Caribbean. The sky was clear and the clusters of stars flickered in the indigo twilight. It had been a month since Lee and Jessica first met and the crisp air blew through her hair. The ocean's waves of the Pacific reflected rippled images of the moon's cream-yellow crescent as they walked the upper deck like it was the edge of space.

"What a beautiful night," Jessica said.

Lee's phone rang and he took it out of his pocket, glanced at it, then put it on silence.

"Sorry about that."

"Why didn't you answer? It might have been important."

"It wasn't. I'm glad you're enjoying your birthday. I wanted this trip to be special, plus I feel the love in the air," Lee grinned.

"Love always needs to be in the air, because we need air to live. And to truly live we need love."

"That's how you feel hunh?"

"Yes. And since we're on the subject, what is your interpretation of love?"

"Um, well I don't believe that love has anything to do with the physical. I also don't think love springs from emotions or feelings either."

"No? Then what is it?" Jessica asked in that Spanish accent Lee found so attractive.

"I was taught by my grandmother that love is the eternal, the true reality that draws and links everything in the universe. So love as I understand it, is the agent of oneness, and when we understand and manifest this spirituality, this love, we become at peace and in harmony with all things. And I believe only in this state can an individual profess to be in love."

"I do agree that true love is spiritual."

Rarely did Jessica find herself in deep conversations with men. But Lee knew how to mentally stimulate her and bring out her inner feelings.

"So what do you think?" Lee asked.

"Love binds man to his spiritual half...his woman. This binding is what makes the two become one, and through this union it is love that manifests oneness."

Lee flashed a subtle smile. "Yeah, that's right."

"Have you ever heard of the ancient myth of the man and woman?'

"No I haven't, what ancient myth is that?"

"My grandmother told it to me when I was a little girl after my grandfather passed away in Puerto Rico. She told me, that once upon a time men and women were one being, not divided into male and female. And at the whim of a god, men and women were split apart. That is why we forever seek our remembered selves in each other...in the hopes of becoming whole once more."

Lee tilted his head toward the sky. "Our grandmother's wisdom."

"Sure is," Jessica agreed.

Lee stared at the heavens for a moment. They began walking towards their cabin for the night in the comfort of silence. When they entered the room, the lighting created an ambience that aroused the animal within them.

Lee pulled his shirt off and Jessica slowly trailed the flats of her fingers across the creases of his abs before they hungrily kissed. They broke their kiss so she could unbutton her blouse, letting it drop to the floor and reached back to unfasten her bra strap. Admiring her breasts gleaming from the lamp, Lee felt dizzy with anticipation. He fantasized of Jessica ever since New York, and now he could have her all over again taking the fantasy past the outer limits of his mind.

Lee wrapped his arms around Jessica's waist, slid the palms of his hands inside the back of her jeans, and gripped her butt to pull her close. He buried the side of his face in the hallow curve of her neck and shoulder with his lips. "Your skin is so soft."

"Ohh God," her voice trembled.

"Are you ready for this?" Lee whispered while he nibbled on her ear.

A sense of peace settled over Lee's heart like a rainbow rests upon the earth with its arch lost in heaven. And for a brief moment he didn't want to move, only to hold her close. He balled his left hand into a fist and placed it beneath her chin to tilt her face so he could kiss the throbbing pulse at the center of her neck. Then slipped his tongue in her mouth. He breathed in her breath and could taste the sweet moisture before combining it with his own. Eventually, Lee's lips left Jessica's mouth to feast on her chin and jawline. As he did so, he grabbed her around the waist and gently laid her on the bed, hovering his broad body over her.

Lee covered her lips with his once more, feeling the firmness of her breast brush against his nipple. Gripping the beltline of Jessica's jeans, he slid her pants down and tossed them on the side of the bed. He reached inside the front of her panties and touched, then trailed his fingers through her thick mound until he felt the wetness of her lips, spreading them apart through the matted hair.

"I want you so badly," Jessica moaned when Lee eased his middle finger inside of her. He slipped his finger out to pull the side of her panties down her thighs and around her ankles. Then unbuckled his belt to remove his slacks along with his briefs and threw them on the floor.

Lee put Jessica's hands above her head and brushed his warm tongue against her collarbone, back and forth in whisper-soft movements that teased and tormented. She arched her back to wrap her legs around his thighs. With his palms flat on the bed and their foreheads touching, he eased inside of her. Jessica opened her legs wide bringing her knees to the sides of her stomach, and Lee pushed himself in so deeply he could feel his testicles against the crease of her fleshly bottom.

The power with which Jessica ground her hips was shocking and Lee couldn't concentrate on anything further, and within seconds his entire body went rigid with the tension of his approaching orgasm. Stronger and stronger he felt the need to release building within him like steam. His first orgasm came within seconds, but he recovered so quickly, he was certain Jessica hadn't noticed.

Determined to give Jessica the same pleasure, Lee began his own eager assault as his hips quickened to a steady but demanding pace. His rhythm increased and he felt her body move with such incredible sweetness beneath him he wanted to scream. But before he did, she squeezed her eyes shut and let out a high-pitched squeal. The expression on Jessica's face made Lee release the most intense burst of semen he'd ever experienced. His stomach muscles locked with each ejaculated squirt until their bodies lay quivering.

Hot sweat rolled down the bridge of Lee's nose like tears as their short pause for breath allowed them to recover. He turned Jessica onto her stomach and hoisted her up by the hips, then entered her from behind and leaned down to kiss the middle of her back through her sweaty hair. Lee reached around to cup her breasts and Jessica reared back. She pushed her buttocks against his groin to suck in every inch of him. Every gesture was filled with meaning and he could feel another orgasm moving within him. At that moment, hot liquid released from the hole of his penis. His cheeks tightened and body stiffened. Together, their bodies communicated a mild, slow-burning rapture that transcended ecstasy.

Lee collapsed on the left side of Jessica with sweat running down the sides of his forehead, and he felt his organ soften. A part of him wanted to stop and absorb the moment, but it was her turn, plus his excitement was still too new, too raw.

Lee began to grow again, feeling the blood pressure increase in equal measures to his heart and manhood, and knew that this moment was far from over. So he turned Jessica on her back again, crawled over the top of her and slid deliciously back inside.

Lee closed his eyes. "You feel so good."

"Ohh, yes," Jessica moaned.

Lee positioned himself on his forearms in a plank to witness the pleasure on her face, and Jessica answered him by clutching the back of his calves with the heels of her feet. Her face turned to the side and she wrapped her arms around his neck and lightly bit into the burning flesh of his shoulder. Jessica's fingers dug into his taut butt cheeks and he felt her shudder…"uunnhh," She spasmed. Jessica held a frozen pose and shook until she collapsed under Lee's embrace.

Lee stroked her cheek, then took his time outlining the soft interior of her lips with the tip of his tongue before kissing her. He was definitely in no hurry; time, like eternity had ceased to exist. He reached down and fondled the moist treasure nestled between her shapely thighs. In the dim lighting it looked like a fresh bloomed flower made of flesh with its petals shiny and twinkling with dew. In its early bud was happiness, and in its full bloom heaven.

Lee pulled Jessica close to his broad chest and held her, feeling her heart beat blindly against his. She clung to him as flesh holds flesh, and the soul holds another. Releasing her, Lee watched a smile slide across her face as she stared at his organ with greedy desire while it grew again.

"I'm ready for you again," Lee whispered.

"Mmm," Jessica purred.

Lee got back on top of her. And as swift as a fleeting shadow, pushed the head of his penis to part her lips. He began gyrating his hips slowly at first, gauging her response until he knew it was time to increase the tempo. Jessica raised her hips to meet and greet his every beat as the friction intensified. They were so close, with their bodies slapping together like a wet hand clap. Timing her movements to push deeper within, Lee eased back then plunged forward as a violent tremor shook the both of them as they clung to one another to reduce the intensity. Their arms and legs were tangled together like they were afraid they might slip away from each other forever if they loosened their hold. Ultimately, they plopped on their backs chasing their breath that escaped and laid there with a ringing sensation in their ears. Suspended in time, their hearts raced to pump blood trying to calm down the aftershocks.

"Wow." Lee turned to Jessica, put his palm on her stomach and kissed her on the shoulder. "Are you okay?" he said in her ear out of breath.

Jessica faced him. "Yes, that was beautiful."

They both lay still, eyes piercing into one another wondering if the conversation they had earlier had any bearing on their lovemaking. It was though their bodies were magnets pulling each other together, and they were thinking the same thing…another round.

Out the corner of Jessica's eye she noticed Lee's phone flashing in his pants pocket lying on the floor, and wondered who would call him at this hour.

* * *

The ship docked in the port of Havana, Cuba and the sun's saffron hue illuminated in that hour of the morning when dawn peeled back. Lee and Jessica were excited to explore the island and there were guides awaiting the arrival of tourists ready to take anyone to the most famous places.

They approached a yellow Ford from the '60s with a chubby dark-skinned Cuban sitting behind the wheel. "Jessica, ask him if he could take us someplace good to eat outside the capital."

"Buenos diás señor, ¿Puede llevarnos a un lugar Bueno para comer a las afueras de la Havána?" The driver nodded and smiled. Lee and Jessica got in and the car began driving west of Havana.

Lee sat back and looked at Jessica. "Thank you."

"You're welcome. How do you know where to go?"

"My cousin used to visit the island a lot, and he told me that the best places to explore were towns outside the capital."

"Oh, does he come here often?"

"Well, right now he's in federal prison. But he'll be out soon."

"Yeah, it's been a long time comin.'"

After a two-hour drive, they arrived at Buena Vista in the Viñales Valley. The scenery was lush green with a distinctive smell of fresh tobacco leaves from the many farms that supplied the cigar shops around the island. They drove past steep-sided rock formations which the countrymen called mogotes. They were covered in green vegetation with the sky powdered greyish-blue above them.

"Isn't that beautiful?" Jessica said.

The driver pulled alongside a roadside stand. Lee and Jessica got out of the vehicle and went to the counter window to read the specials that were handwritten on a chalkboard hanging on the back wall. Cubans crowded the front to watch the cook slather onion slices laced with chili and vinegar onto thin slices of lechón with roasted pork slightly blackened on the edges. They waited in line as the aroma of smoked wood roasting two large pigs on the right side of the stand, wafted towards them.

"That smells delicious," Lee said. "I know, and I'm starving."

When it was their turn Lee ordered two large con lechóns and handed a teenage girl convertible pesos the equivalent of $3.20 U.S. dollars. They began eating when an older lady with white hair tied in a ponytail, brought them a drink contained in a bamboo vessel that was a concoction of aguardiente and ginger, with honey and pepper.

Lee savored the flavor around his tongue before swallowing. "Now, this is scrumptious." Jessica sipped greedily. "Mmm, this is sooo good."

They finished their meals and were anxious to see what else the island had to offer so they returned to the car. Lee paid the driver and asked him to take them to another place to eat. He drove them southeast to the city of Trinidad, a vibrant UNESCO World Heritage site that was polished with rocky roads and a city view of 19th-century Spanish style. As they continued, the Ford drove alongside Spanish horses on their way to Santiago, the cultural and commercial center of the eastern part of the island.

The car stopped at Castillo del Morro, a colonial-era castle that was converted into a restaurant that was perched on a steep hillside. Lee and Jessica exited the car in anticipation of tasting more cultural foods as they entered an area of the front that had tables aligned in rows. In the back against the wall was an old jukebox that played '45 records. They sat down to watch a young man in his twenties who stood five-foot-six and wore a white apron, tend to a fish scored with diagonal cuts sitting in a pan of sizzling garlic. He spooned hot oil on its surface and added octopus to a second pan with oil mingled with sofrito, onion, garlic, cumin, oregano, and bay leaf. The aromas made love to Lee and Jessica's noses causing their taste buds to salivate. The chef brought them two plates.

After satisfying their stomachs and ready to return to the cruise liner, they drove back through Trinidad and stopped at the famous Palacio de Valle restaurant with its gorgeous Cienfuegos structure. The dining hall was luxurious with high ceilings, marble pillars, and silk drapes cascading the windows. Poetry was carved into the structure in gold Arabic and Spanish calligraphy.

Lee looked around. "I never would've known Cuba was so beautiful. The American media outlets never show these places about the island."

"I know; this place is amazing."

"Let's sit next to the window."

Lee and Jessica sat at a table and were ready to eat again when a woman in her mid '50s with salt-and-pepper hair wearing a see-through hairnet, asked if they wanted to try something special. They said yes and the woman disappeared into the kitchen. She returned after a few minutes with two platters of seared pork fillets in a savory cacao sauce. She left again and came back with two bowls containing ripe plantains formed into small dumplings stewed in a rich green coconut-milk sauce.

Jessica sniffed her food. "I think Cuban food is now my favorite."

"It sure has moved to the top of my list," Lee smiled.

When they finished eating Lee gave the lady a tip before he and Jessica went back out to the guide who was listening to a baseball game over the radio. The evening was young and it would be a couple of hours before they got back to their cabin on the ship, and they had other ideas in mind once they got there.

Lee's phone kept illuminating through his front pants pocket from incoming calls, which he was ignoring. He saw that Jessica noticed.

"Aren't you going to answer that?"

Lee took the phone out of his pocket to see who was calling before he let it go to voicemail, and Jessica caught a glimpse at the screen. The name read Percilla with a picture. Who was Percilla she wondered?

CHAPTER 10

Lee hung up the phone stunned by the news he just received as he sat on the couch in his Victorian townhouse in Baldwin Hills. He got up to walk up the stairs of the boxy two-story building where the floor plan narrowed and paced back and forth on the second floor. He then went to the inner sanctum of the house which had his office and an adjacent parlor, so he could gather his thoughts. Now, he understood why Percilla was trying to reach him while he was in Cuba. If he had just taken the call he would have found out that Chris was ill and in the hospital dying, and he could have gotten into Miami and taken a flight to Arizona.

Lee walked through the hallway to his bedroom and scanned across his pale gray walls of framed pictures of Malcom X, Nelson Mandela, and Nat Turner, reflecting on all the turning points of his life. Opening the closet, he pulled clothes off the hanger and laid them over the arm of one of the six-piece collections of fiberglass chairs, got his Louis Vuitton travel bag, and began packing. When he was done, he called an Uber to take him to the airport.

In less than an hour Lee arrived at Arizona's Sky Harbor International Airport. He disembarked the plane, went through the terminal to get his luggage and saw Percilla sitting in the lounge waiting. When he approached her, she sprung forward and leapt into his arms. He dropped his bag. "It's gonna be okay," Lee said as he squeezed her.

"I just can't believe it," Percilla wept. She buried her Face in Lee's chest. They gathered themselves and walked out the front doors to the parking garage where Percilla was parked.

It had been nearly two years since they last saw each other and the ride to Scottsdale was silent with only the sounds of Percilla's sniffles. When they pulled into the driveway of the Priest's, she turned the engine off and just sat there teary-eyed staring at Lee. They both couldn't believe Chris was dead.

The next morning Lee, Percilla, and the Priests' along with other family members attended Chris's funeral service. Afterwards, at the burial Lee noticed Mr. Priest talking to two men who were standing away from everyone else. When the memorial was over and everyone got into their vehicles to leave the cemetery, the two men followed them, then turned in a different direction. Lee turned to Percilla. "Who were those men?"

"That was Mr. Priest's lawyer and a private toxicologist he hired to reexamine Chris's body tissue."

"Why does he want Chris's body reexamined?"

"Because he thinks Chris's ex-girlfriend might have had something to do with it."

"Are you serious?"

"Yes, so he wants to make sure there was no foul play."

"But didn't they already do all of the tests when the autopsy was done?"

"Yes. But Mr. Priest is paying for a more comprehensive test to be conducted."

The private examiner brought in special equipment that the county coroner's lab didn't have, in order to retest Chris's blood samples using forensic science. Once placed under a microscope, the tests revealed that in all samples there were traces found of a deadly poison called polonium 210. An odorless and tasteless substance that in small amounts could kill a human being within a week if ingested. The evidence was presented to the District Attorney's Office and Mr. Priest told the D.A. about Chris's pregnant ex-girlfriend Trisha, and her reaction to Chris breaking up with her.

* * *

For the past two years Trisha worked as a bartender during the night at a small tavern in Scottsdale. During that time, she had become very close friends with her co-worker Mila. Trisha told Mila about her pregnancy with Chris's child and how volatile their relationship had gotten.

"Mila, I'll be right back, cover for me, I have to go to the restroom." Trisha quick-stepped from behind the bar and into the lady's room, opened the middle stall, pulled her red hair back, and leaned over the toilet to vomit. After several minutes she returned behind the counter, face flushed red, only a shade lighter than the freckles around her cheeks.

"Are Ya okay?" Mila asked.

"I'm fine, I just had a little morning sickness. Don't know why it's called morning sickness though," she groaned.

The two giggled.

The night was slow, so Trisha and Mila began wiping tables and putting away empty glasses into the back dishwasher. Their shift was about to end, so they finished cleaning and refilling the peanut trays before they left.

"Ya wanna get somethin' to eat?" Mila said as they were walking out the door into the parking lot.

"I'm not really hungry. But I do have a craving for ice cream."

"Let's go to Dairy Queen."

They both got in their cars and Trisha followed Mila to the nearest Dairy Queen. When they walked in and went to the register, Mila ordered two banana splits with hot fudge and they went to a table.

Trisha sat down. "Thanks."

Mila took a seat across from Trisha and tucked the string of black hair behind her ear that came out of its ponytail. "So how are ya really doin'? It seems like somethin' is botherin' ya because you've been actin' kinda' weird."

"Girl, I'm just a little upset because Chris and I have been arguing a lot ever since I asked him if we were getting married. We have been together off and on ever since college, and I feel like he doesn't want to tie himself down now that he received that big management position at his father's firm. Plus, he is always around women; rich women," Trisha griped.

"How do ya know that's the reason?"

"Well, last week him, his father, and other business associates attended a fundraiser ball, and the day after I went to his house. When he got in the shower I went into his bedroom and found one of his shirts laying across the chair at his desk with lipstick on the collar."

"So ya think he's cheatin' on ya?"

"I hope not, but I believe he is because he's done it in the past."

They ate their banana splits while Trisha stared out the window in deep thought.

"Trish, it'll be okay."

"I guess so. I'm ready to go home, I'm tired."

"Okay." They got up and threw their empty containers in the trash before they left.

The following night at work Trisha was quiet until a beer mug slipped out of her hand that fell to the floor and shattered. "Shit!"

"Trish, ya okay?" Mila bent down to help her pick up the broken pieces of glass.

"I'm fine," she grumbled.

"Ya sure? Cause ya aint said a word all night."

"When we left the Dairy Queen last night something told me to swing by Chris's. As I drove up the street to the house, I had my headlights off. Girl, do you know what I saw?"

"What?"

"Chris with a tall blonde who was wearing a white pants suit. They were standing on the sidewalk kissing."

"What did ya do?"

"I just made a U-turn and left."

"That's fucked up,"

"Girl, that's not the half of it."

"What do ya mean?"

"This morning I went to his office and confronted him with what I saw, and you know what he said?"

"Don't tell me he denied it."

"No girl, he said we were over and that I don't have to worry about taking care of a child. I can just live my life."

"Are ya serious, what the hell does that supposed to mean?"

"He's going to try and take my baby, and his family has all sorts of high-priced lawyers. I don't know what I'm going to do."

"Trish, ya deserve better than what he's puttin' ya through. Especially after all the shit he's done in the past."

"You're right, I do deserve better."

Trisha continued working throughout the night contemplating what she should do. One thing was certain, she'd be damned if she let him take her baby.

Later that night before Trisha's shift ended, Chris entered the tavern and went to the counter where she was serving a customer. "Trisha, I need to speak with you when you get off work."

"Okay. Do you want a drink?"

"Um, let me get a Blanton's Bourbon." Trisha got the bottle from the shelf and poured Chris a drink wondering what he wanted to talk about. Chris sat down and enjoyed his drink while he waited for her shift to end.

Mila left from behind the counter to go home. "Bye Trish, I'll see ya tomorrow, call me."

"So…where do you want to go and talk?" Trisha folded the towel she used to clean with, and laid it under the shelf.

"Follow me to Starbucks, we can talk over coffee," Chris said.

Chris and Trisha left the bar and drove only a few blocks until they pulled into the parking lot of a Starbucks. Once inside, Chris ordered two large Frappuccino's and they sat at a table in the corner of the shop.

"So, what's on your mind Chris ?"

"I don't know how to tell you this other than to just come out and say it , I'm getting married."

"Married! Married to who?"

"That's not important. What's important, is she's also pregnant with my child and I want both of my children to live under one roof."

Trisha couldn 't believe what she was hearing. *The nerve of him*, she thought. She sat quiet for a moment and t ook a sip of coffee before responding. "So, what does that mean?" Although she knew what it meant, she didn't want to hear the answer.

"Look Trisha, how about I deposit $200,000 dollars into your account, and you sign over full custody to me once the baby is born. I'll give you visitation, that way you'll be able to live your life free of motherhood."

Trisha wanted to scream. She felt the blood pressure in her forehead rise as she looked at Chris and realized that he felt everything he had just said was normal. *What an arrogant son of a bitch*, she thought. Trisha knew at that moment what had to be done. He must pay much more than $200,000 dollars. He must pay with something that was priceless. His life.

The following morning Trisha called Mila to meet her at Coronado Park in Scottsdale.

"Hey Trish."

"Hi girl." The two hugged and Mila could see something was wrong.

"So what's up? I know you didn't call me here for a stroll in the park."

"You're right . Girl, I've been up all night thinking about this."

"Thinkin' about what ?"

"How I want to get rid of Chris."

"Get rid of him how?"

"So he won't be able to take my baby. That son of a bitch offered me $200,000 dollars to sign over custody, can you believe that?"

"He had the nerve to offer ya money?"

"Yes. So I want his ass gone forever."

"Calm down and lower your voice." Mila looked around to make sure no one heard them.

"I'm serious, I want him dead," Trisha whispered.

"Let's go to the bench over there."

The two went and sat down.

"He's got another thing coming if he thinks I'm going to give up my baby."

"Emotions are takin' over ya right now because of ya hormones."

"No, I'm serious. I have a little over $15,000 saved." Again, Mila turned and looked behind them.

"If ya sure, I can talk to my brother. He knows people; bad people."

"Yes, talk to him."

"Okay, I'll see what I can do and call you later." The two got up from the bench and walked back to their cars in silence.

* * *

Mila's t w in br ot her Vladamir was in the U. S. Army. He had just returned to the States from South Korea, where he had spent nine-months on assignment at the Army base in the city of Pusan. While stationed there, Vladamir would frequently visit the many massage parlors and prostitute glasshouses. Although he and Mila were born in America, their parents immigrated from Russia. Vladamir associated with people who had a major Russian influential presence in the underworld of the city of Pusan. This underworld was rife with organized crime, and so it was easy to obtain deadly substances.

Vladamir was able to get a bottle of poison in an eye drop bottle, from one of the prostitutes he saw regularly, and snuck it on a U.S. military flight back to Luke Airforce Base in Arizona.

Three weeks had passed since Trisha and Mila met at the park. They sat in the car and looked out the window to make sure no one could see them when Mila took a sealed baggy out of her purse that contained a visine bottle full of clear liquid.

Mila handed Trisha the bag. "This is deadly poison. My brother said all ya have to do is put a couple of drops in Chris's drink."

"Only a couple?" Trisha asked to make certain it would be enough.

"Yeah, but be careful not to get any on ya skin."

Ten minutes before Trisha's shift began, she put the baggy in her purse, and got her iPhone to call Chris. She told him to come to her job so she could sign the paperwork.

Chris entered the bar 30 minutes later, went to the counter where Trisha was working and sat down on a stool. Trisha put an empty glass in front of him. "What do you w ant to drink ?"

"A Wild Turkey on the rocks will be fine."

I 'll bring it over to the table so we can talk."

"Alright."

Trisha had her purse on the shelf under the counter. When Chris got up to go to a table, she quickly reached into it and grabbed the baggy with the visine bottle. She got a glass, lowered it below the counter and squeezed three squirts of poison into it, then filled it with bourbon. Her heart was thumping and hands shaking to the point she thought she'd give herself away. Trisha took a deep breath and took the drink over to Chris where he was waiting.

"Here you go. Excuse me for a minute, I have to go to the ladies room."

Trisha threw the bottle in the trash that was clutched in her fist, then let out a long exhale. She washed her trembling hands and knew she had to calm herself before going back out, so she splashed water on her face and pulled a few paper towels from the dispensary to dry with. When she went back out to sit at the table across from Chris, he had a document laid out.

"Are you okay ?" Chris ask d, before he took a swig from his glass.

"I'm fine, let me see that." Trisha picked up the paper and pretended to read long enough for Chris to drink most of the bourbon.

Chris pointed to the signature line. "All you have to do is sign at the bottom."

"I can't do it !" Trisha threw the document at his ches t and got up to leave.

Chris grabbed her arm. "You' ll hear from my lawyer and I'll make you look like you're unfit to raise a child."

Trisha didn't care. The deed was done. And there was nothing Chris could do about it now. Over the next five days, Chris fell extremely ill and was admitted to the hospital. He lost half his body weight and all his hair and doctors couldn't explain his condition from the tests they conducted. Then, one late afternoon while he was asleep, his organs shut down and he died.

* * *

The Chris's case was reopened and ruled a homicide. Detectives put Trisha under surveillance and would go into the tavern to order beers. They noticed that she and her co-worker Mila would hang out during their time off work, so investigators decided to look into Mila's background.

One morning Trisha got into her car and drove to a nearby Safeway unaware she was being tailed. She reached in her purse to get her lip gloss and realized she forgot to discard the empty baggy that held the visine bottle. She pulled into an alley next to a garbage dumpster and tossed the bag in it. Detectives waited until she drove away before retrieving the clear Ziplock which contained a top to an eye drop bottle. They took it to the forensic crime lab to be dusted for fingerprints and examined with the same specialized equipment used to retest Chris s blood samples. The results came back positive for trace amounts of polonium 210 and A warrant was issued for Trisha's arrest.

When investigators subpoenaed Trisha's phone and bank records, they discovered that Mila's brother Vladamir had received $5,000 dollars that was deposited via wire transfer from Trisha's bank account, shortly after Chris became ill.

Confronted in the interrogation room, Trisha realized that the evidence was mounting against her and she faced a possible death sentence for first degree premeditated murder. She quickly implicated Mila and V ladamir , and they were both picked up and charged with conspiracy to murder. All three were in the Maricopa County Jail for nearly six months.

Once their trial began it lasted eight days and the jury took four hours to reach guilty verdicts on all counts. Two weeks later Trisha was sentenced to 25 years to life. For Mila's testimony she was given a reduced sentence of 18 years, and Vladamir received 10 years with a separate additional federal sentence of 180 months for smuggling a deadly substance through military transport.

Trisha returned to the cell that felt like a refrigerator from the cold air blowing through the vent against cement and metal. She laid on the bottom bunk and wrapped herself in the itchy wool blanket and cried. Eight months pregnant and convicted of murder, she was gripped by the fear of her baby growing up without her as she felt the baby move. And as it grew, so did her anger.

Every morning a nurse named Ms. Turner would bring around Trisha's daily pre-natal care vitamins through the food-tray slot. "How are you feeling today?"

Trisha sighed. "I guess I'm okay."

"I'm so sorry that you have to go through this. If you need anything, you best let me know."

"Okay." Trisha swallowed the pills and took a sip of water from the sink. Nurse Turner closed the trap and left.

Later that evening detention officers escorted Trisha to the medical ward for a routine exam, and nurse Turner sat her in a chair to check her blood pressure. "Everything checks out fine. Darling, the baby can feel what you're going through."

"I know, I just can't believe this is happening."

"Dear, let God take care of it and it will all be fine."

"I guess you're right. Thank you for being so nice to me."

"You deserve to be treated fairly, you just made a horrible mistake."

"I know a secret that would probably change things."

"Darling , if you ever need to talk, I'm here."

"Thanks."

"Here comes the doctor, I'll see you when I bring your vitamins."

"Okay."

The following morning nurse Turner made her rounds to deliver medications and s topped at Trisha's cell. "Here you go dear, are you feeling alright?"

"Yes, I'm fine."

"Good darling, because we want the baby to be nice and healthy."

"I just haven't been able to get much sleep."

"I know you're going through some pretty difficult times right now, but you have to get your rest for the baby's sake, sweetie."

Trisha kneeled and put her face to the opening of the slot. "Do you know what Chris told me?"

Nurse Turner leaned down. "What sweetie?"

"That he and his fat her ha d $75 million dollars stashed in Switzerland from illegal stock selling that no one knows about."

"Oh dear."

"And he said, not even his mother knows."

"Darling, I think you should alert the authorities because you could use that information to probably ensure that your parents get the baby."

"Do you think so?"

"Yes sweetie."

"Okay , thanks." Trisha rose from the trap and stood to look out the window of the door.

Nurse Turner gave her a grin and winked before she left.

Trisha called her attorney the following day, who notified the FBI, and she was interviewed at the jail. Based on her statements federal investigators looked into any suspicious wire transfers from CP Financial and found large amounts of money going overseas to an investment holding company named Pristine Equities. With that information the Securities and Exchange Commission launched an investigation into securities fraud.

The SEC discovered that CP Fi nanc ials ' ac count ing records a nd f inanc ial rep ort s t o it s self-regulatory organization, the National Association of Securities Dealers, were manipulated in order to transfer unaccounted funds to Switzerland. Federal agents served Mr. Priest with a search warrant and combed through files of paperwork, confiscating all of the firm's hard drives.

The investigation revealed that Mr. Priest hired interns that he took through trading training courses to work in his online chat rooms. Management would give the rookie brokers a client-list to issue buy recommendations, tricking clients into purchasing micro-cap low-volume stocks. CP Financial owned large blocks of these shares and would sell them when the buying pressure increased due to the recommendations. This assured profits as management would purchase more stock to pump up the share price, then dump them onto unsuspecting clients that could not resell them in the open market once the price collapsed.

SEC investigators found that millions of dollars had been transferred into crypto currency held by Pristine Equities that was domiciled in the territorial district of Zurich. When the authorities in Switzerland were contacted, the FBI was informed that Pristine Equities was a shell corporation with no business operations and the assets were held in a Trust account with Credit Suisse Bank.

CHAPTER 11

It was the morning after the funeral and Lee was back in L.A. at his office having a telephonic meeting with one of his new clients.

"Now, about the specifics of futures. There is a subgroup of traders called commercial hedgers. These individuals or entities, usually corporations, use long side bullish, or produce short side bearish, the commodities that they hedge. Major livestock producers hedge their feed usage by going long on the corn market and sell their meat production by selling live cattle futures contracts for delivery. And oil refineries go long crude oil to stabilize or average the price of oil and deliver against short, gasoline and heating futures contracts, called the crack spread."

"Okay, I can see their hedging strategies," the client said.

"Also, an entity using copper such as manufacturers for jewelry, wheat for cereal makers, or any other commodity can lock in costs to stabilize its business by using futures contracts, and options contracts on futures. There are two Commodities Options Trade reports; one covers open interest, which is the net futures positions remaining open at the end of the week on Friday at 3:30 p.m. eastern, and the second report details open options contracts. So it's important for us to study those reports because the holders of those contracts are mostly large corporations that need or produce the commodities. Those corporations have excellent intelligence and great trading experience. Therefore, if the census is pronouncedly bullish or bearish, it is a strong clue to where the market is headed. Those types of traders are hedged; they are on both sides of the market and are not affected, except for lost opportunity if the market goes up or down," Lee explained.

Nicole opened the door and stuck her head in Lee's office. "There's someone here to see you," she whispered.

Lee nodded and held up his index finger for her to give him a minute.

"As I was saying, those corporations are well financed. That is what is meant when you hear analysts say, the commodity is held in strong hands. Weak hands refer to the average traders with naked or unhedged positions. We also look for signs in copper because it is the best barometer of financial activity. As its price rises, so does the economy, and when its price retracts, so does the stock market. Because it is used in so many products it's pretty much all over the place, making demand for it a sign of economic growth."

"Sounds good Mr. Prince, and I feel confident in having my money in your hands."

"I appreciate it, and we place extreme value in managing your account. You have a nice day and I'll email you all the necessary paperwork this afternoon."

"Thank you, Mr. Prince. You have a good day as well. Goodbye."

Lee got up from his chair and walked out into the hallway where two men dressed in dark blue suits were seated. One of them had a briefcase lying across his lap.

"Hi, how can I help you gentlemen?"

"Mr. Lee Prince?" The man with the briefcase said.

"Yes, that's me."

"Can we talk in private?"

"Sure, come into my office." The two men followed Lee and closed the door behind them. "Please have a seat."

"Thank you," they both said.

"Now, what can I do for you?" Lee said.

"Mr. Prince we are federal agents conducting an investigation into securities violations during the time you worked at CP Financial," the agent with the briefcase said.

Lee was unaware that an investigation was underway into illegal security practices at Mr. Priest's firm, nor did he know this conduct was taking place at the time he and Chris worked there. The agents questioned Lee concerning activities he may have participated in while working in CP Financial's chat rooms. He told investigators he had no knowledge of any unethical activities nor illegal sales practices. After several minutes they concluded their questions and the agent with the briefcase opened it, took out an envelope, and handed it to Lee.

"What is this?"

"This is a subpoena to appear before a federal grand jury." Lee removed the paper that was inside along with a round trip plane ticket and looked at both agents without blinking.

"Why would I have to appear before a grand jury?"

"Because we need your testimony under oath sir."

"This flight is scheduled for Monday. That's pretty short notice."

"Well, we have to move the case along. You enjoy the rest of your day Mr. Prince." The two men got up to leave and the agent without the briefcase gave Lee a card with their contact information.

Lee crouched in his chair, took a deep breath, closed his eyes and exhaled. He noticed the lingering scent of cheap cologne the agents left behind as he placed the palms of his hands behind his head and locked his fingers.

A knock on the door interrupted his thoughts and Ashtiyani peaked her head in. "Lee is everything okay?"

"Yeah, come in and close the door behind you."

"Who were those two men?" she asked.

"They were federal securities investigators talking to me about fraudulent securities practices at a firm I used to work for back when I was still in college."

"Securities fraud?"

"They said the company I worked for, CP Financial, was engaging in a pump-and-dump scheme that stretches back several years."

"What does that have to do with you?"

"The agents claim that Mr. Priest, my friend Chris's father, possibly had us issue buy recommendations of certain stocks the firm already owned. Once clients purchased shares driving up the price, CP Financial would sell their blocks of stock knowing the price would collapse and clients would be unable to sell because of low demand. The stocks were pretty much illiquid."

"So what's going to happen to you?"

"Well, I have to go to Arizona. They issued me a subpoena to appear before a grand jury on Monday."

"Next week? So what do you need me to do?"

"You and Nicole handle things here at CYGNUS, and I'll keep you two updated. Also, check with Eduardo on the status of those properties. I'm going home for the day."

"Okay, I'll take care of it."

Lee got his briefcase, threw the envelope inside, then grabbed his suit jacket from the coat rack and left his office with Ashtiyani. While walking through the hall toward the elevators, his phone buzzed. "Hello."

"You have a collect call from… 'Yusuf,' an inmate at the Lompoc, California Federal Correctional Facility. Press…"

Lee accepted the call before the computerized voice could finish.

"What's up fam?" Lee said.

"How you doin' relative?" Yusuf greeted.

"It's all good, just movin' CYGNUS to the next level. How you been in there?"

"Aww aint nothing,' just can't wait to finally be out of this cage. You know a bird is meant to fly, plus I'm ready to join CYGNUS and the team."

"Yeah, and we're all ready for you too. I'll have everything set up so Nicole can mentor you through the ninja trader software and level II quote systems."

"Man, I can't wait to finally be able to put this MBA to use outside of here. Even though I've been able to grow my E*Trade account through snail methods."

"Yeah fam, aint nothin' like real time."

"I know that's right. What's up with Jahi? I haven't talked to him in nearly a week."

"He's good. You know how your son is, always busy studying."

"I hope you know how much I appreciate everything you've done for him."

"Man, he's like my nephew, and you're my relative. I just did what I was supposed to."

"I'm just grateful you ain't in here with me."

"I know, I easily could've been too."

"I know that's right, because we put major work back in the day. But you made somethin' of yourself. Well, I'ma let you tend to your business, and I'll hit you again in a few days, I just wanted to say what's up."

"Alright fam, you stay safe."

"Much love relative."

Yusuf had less than a year on his sentence and Lee didn't want to concern him with what was taking place, plus he felt he hadn't done anything wrong. He only discussed the upside potentialities of investments and never tricked anyone.

The elevator door opened, and Lee stepped inside.

* * *

The following morning Lee returned to his office to find Ashtiyani waiting for him.

"Good morning," Lee said as he laid his briefcase on top of his desk. Ashtiyani closed the door. "I don't know if I can work with Nicole."

"What do you mean?"

"I've been a part of this team longer than her and she already acts like she's running things around here."

Right at that moment, Nicole walked in with an envelope in her hand. "Excuse me guys, Lee this came in the mail yesterday after you left. It's from the SEC."

Lee took the envelope, read what was inside, then slapped it on his desk and plopped in his chair.

"Lee, what's wrong?" Ashtiyani asked.

"The SEC is temporarily suspending my license until further notice."

Nicole and Ashtiyani looked at each other. "Are you serious," Nicole said under her breath.

"Ladies could you please give me a few minutes?"

"Sure," they both said. Ashtiyani and Nicole left the office and closed the door.

Lee got up from behind his desk and went to the window overlooking Downtown Los

Angeles. The morning rays reflected off the glass skyscrapers. He sat back down and pulled out the bottom drawer of his desk where he kept a bottle of Hennessey. He got a glass, poured himself a drink and swirled around in the chair to look out the window again at the skyline. His phone buzzed. "Hello."

After a few minutes on the phone he hung up, refilled his glass to the rim, and took a huge swallow that made him clench his teeth and close his eyes. Jessica told him she was pregnant. She said it happened when they were on their cruise and waited until now to tell him because of everything he was going through with the death of his friend.

Jahi opened the door and looked in. "Unc, you okay?"

"Yeah I'm good."

"You sure?" Jahi could see the stress on Lee's face and the glass of liquor on the desk. "I just found out from Jessica that I'm gonna be a father."

"Isn't that great news?"

"I guess so. But I also just received notice that my security license is temporarily suspended."

"What?"

"I can no longer manage any accounts until I can clear all of this up."

"It'll work itself out unc, you didn't do anything wrong."

"I know. But I'm gonna have to demote my title with the firm to consultant until everything is resolved with the SEC."

"Well, just let me know what to do and I'll help pick up the slack."

"Nicole will meet with everyone."

"Okay, but congratulations."

Lee stayed in his office the entire morning until he decided to go someplace to eat. He went out the door and noticed a white woman with brunette hair and a cleanshaven Asian man leaving with Ashtiyani. He called Nicole over. "Who are those two people Ashtiyani is leaving with?"

"I don't know. But they were talking in her office and then they all left without Ashtiyani saying anything."

"Let me know when she comes back."

"Okay, I will."

That looked strange, Lee thought. On his way to the elevators he dialed LAX to book a flight to Phoenix, then called Percilla.

"Hey, how are you? I'll be in town on Sunday, my flight lands at 10:00 a.m."

When Lee hung up, he couldn't shake the odd feeling he had of seeing Ashtiyani leave with those two individuals. He just decided to go home.

The next morning Lee saw Ashtiyani walk by his office door and called her. "Ashtiyani come in and close the door."

"What's up?"

"I noticed you leave yesterday with two people I have never seen before, is everything alright?"

Ashtiyani looked at Lee for a few seconds before she spoke. "That was Homeland Security."

"What?" Lee's eyebrows raised forming wrinkles in his forehead. "What would Homeland Security want with you?"

"They wanted to talk to me about my financial contributions to the Fakka Foundation."

"Why would Homeland Security come to your place of business to talk about donations?"

"They said everyone who donated would be talked to, and that it was only routine because the Palestinian government is considered a terrorist group."

"Routine? Sounds like profiling to me. So, is everything straight?"

"Yes, I just went with the agents to the federal building down the street to give a formal statement."

That sounded strange to Lee. But he had other concerns to contend with. "Alright, as long as everything is good. I already have a lot going on around here and I need everyone's focus."

"Everything is fine."

Ashtiyani got up to leave, and Nicole came in behind her. "Lee, do you need me to hold a special board meeting?"

"Yeah, send out the notices and hold it on Monday. I'll be in Arizona so hold a proxy vote retitling me to a consultation position."

"Okay, is there anything else?"

"Yeah there is, make sure Ashtiyani is okay, she doesn't seem right."

"Lee, that's another thing I wanted to talk to you about."

"What's that?"

"I feel like Ashtiyani has a problem with how I do things around here."

"Why do you think that?"

"Because she kinda got an attitude when I asked her for CYGNUS' last quarterly report so I could evaluate earning to game for this quarter's earnings percentage increase goal. She kept coming up with reasons not to show them to me."

"Alright, don't worry I'll get them to you."

Once Nicole left Lee pulled the top drawer of his desk open and took out the congratulations card Percilla mailed him once CYGNUS Investments was launched. He re-read the quote she wrote by Dr. Wayne Dyer: "The basics of belief in synchronicity are that every single life has a purpose and a deeper meaning than we are generally aware of. Behind all form is an intelligence that is exquisitely perfect, and that works in synchronized fashion. Everything happens for a purpose, and the puzzle pieces of life fit together perfectly. When you trust and know these thoughts, you will daily recognize evidence for your belief in synchronicity."

CHAPTER 12

Lee's flight landed at Sky Harbor International Airport and he exited the terminal to go outside to find a taxi that would take him to Downtown Phoenix. The cab drove him to a Hilton Resort where he called Percilla to let her know where he was staying. The hotel room smelled of fresh lilac and violet and the cool A.C. made him kick off his loafers and plop on the thick mattress. He stared at the cream ceiling for what seemed like only a few minutes before nodding off to sleep. He slept the rest of the day and throughout the night until Monday morning. After he got up to take a steaming shower and got dressed, he went to the dining room to get a continental breakfast of waffles, eggs, and coffee.

While Lee was eating, he noticed out the corner of his eye, a bald-headed white man wearing round wire-framed glasses sitting at the corner table staring at him. After finishing breakfast, he dialed an Uber and went to the parking lot to wait. The car arrived and took him to the federal court building only a few blocks from the hotel. Lee went inside to the front desk where a woman wearing too much makeup sat behind a computer pecking away on a keyboard. She looked up when he approached and Lee could see the line where her foundation ended along her jaw, her face a darker shade than her neck. Tight curls streamed over both shoulders and her dark hair was teased in the front. "May I help you, sir?"

"Yes, I have an appointment." Lee handed her the subpoena.

"Please have a seat." The receptionist picked up the phone and placed a call. "Mr. Prince, take the elevator to the third floor and go down the hall to jury room number two."

When Lee got to the front entrance of the jury room the door was open. Standing at an oval table was a short Jewish man in his late '50s dressed in a grey suit with a long black beard, wearing a black yarmulke. He was flipping through paperwork when he looked and saw Lee standing in the doorway. "Mr. Prince?"

Lee entered the room. "Yes, that's me. And you are…"

"I'm Joseph Steinbrenner, here to represent you. How are you?" He shook Lee's hand. "I'm okay I guess. Who sent you to represent me?"

"Sir, Mr. Priest hired me to be your attorney to ensure your rights are protected in these and any future proceedings. All you are required to do at this deposition is to answer a few questions under oath, which shouldn't take long at all."

A federal U.S. District and SEC attorney entered the room with a nine-panel grand jury, federal judge, and a transcriber. They all took seats at the table.

The deposition took less than an hour before concluding and Mr. Steinbrenner advised Lee not to discuss the case with anyone, and that he would be updated on any developments. Lee exited the building and called Percilla.

"Hello," Percilla answered.

"Hi, meet me at the Starbucks around the corner from the court building."

"Okay, I'll see you in a few minutes."

Lee strolled down the sidewalk reflecting on all the questions he was asked. The mid- morning sun was gaining strength even in the shadows of the skyscrapers. He crossed the street to a food cart to buy a bottle of water and saw a homeless man pushing a shopping cart filled with clothes.

"Excuse me sir, here you go." Lee gave the man a $20 dollar bill. "Oh, thank you so much. God bless you," the homeless man said.

"You're welcome, you have a nice day." Lee continued on his way to the Starbucks. By the time he arrived in the parking lot, Percilla was already waiting in her car with the driver's-side window down.

"Lee, over here," Percilla shouted. She got out, left the door open, and scampered to him.

They hugged each other. "Hi, how did you get here so fast?"

"I was already driving to this side of town. How did it go?"

"Let's get some coffee and I'll tell you about it." They went to Percilla's car so she could close the door, then went into the coffee shop. When they walked up to the counter Lee ordered two espressos and they went and sat at a table next to the front door.

"So, are you okay?" Percilla asked.

"Yeah, I'm good. Do you know a woman named Gisselle Helmsmith?"

"No. Why, who is that?"

"While they were questioning me about the methods of our sales practices at Mr.

Priest's firm, they made mention of a Gisselle Helsmith who lives in Switzerland."

"I've never heard of her. But I have heard Chris mention Switzerland before he got sick."

"They asked me if I knew about a firm named Pristine Equities that was held in a Trust, with Gisselle Helmsmith as the beneficiary."

"So, what does all of this mean for you and Mr. Priest?"

"I'm not sure yet. The lawyer Mr. Priest hired to represent me said he'd contact me in a week or so."

They both sipped their coffee and Percilla's eyes watered. "I pray you overcome this," she whispered.

Lee's phone rang. "Excuse me a second, hello…okay, bye."

"Lee, is everything alright?"

Lee shook his head. "I don't know, my C.I.O. just told me Homeland Security was at the firm with a search warrant. I have to get back to L.A."

"Why would Homeland Security be at your firm?"

"I'm pretty sure it has to do with my executive Ashtiyani. Could you take me to the resort so I can get my luggage, and then drop me off at the airport?"

"Of course."

On their way to the hotel Lee noticed a Navy-blue Toyota Camry through the passenger side view mirror following them. He swore the same car drove by him when he was walking to meet Percilla. But as soon as they turned into the parking lot of the Hilton the car kept going. His mind must be playing tricks on him, he thought.

* * *

Lee arrived back in Los Angeles, where Nicole, Ashtiyani, and Jahi were waiting for him.

Agents seized all CYGNUS Investments' computer hard drives out of Ashtiyani's office because she was Executive Secretary and Treasurer responsible for the firm's books and accounting records.

"What the hell happened? I thought all you did was donate to charity." Lee crossed his arms.

Ashtiyani sat on the edge of the chair in Lee's office with her palms over her knees. She looked up at Lee with glossed over eyes. "That is all I did, like I told you before."

"Then why did Homeland Security confiscate your computers and CYGNUS' financial records?"

"I don't know," Ashtiyani said in a low tone, then put her head down.

"Tomorrow I'll go see what all this is about. For now, just go home for the day."

"Alright," she sighed.

"Nicole, I need to talk to you in private."

Ashtiyani shot Nicole a piercing look before she walked out the door.

"Do you need me to go with you tomorrow?" Nicole asked.

"No, I'll be fine. But until I find out what's goin' on, I need you to oversee all of the accounts."

"Sure, don't worry."

The following afternoon Lee went to the FBI building in the Los Angeles Downtown District. He gave the secretary at the front desk his name and she made a phone call. The male

Asian agent who escorted Ashtiyani out of her office appeared with a brown file clutched in his hand. "Mr. Prince, could you come with me sir?" Lee followed the agent into an interview room with a one-way mirror. "Please have a seat, would you like anything to drink?"

"No thank you, I'm fine."

The agent left Lee in the cold room for several minutes before returning with a red-head female whose hair was pulled into a ponytail.

She sat a recorder on the table. "Good afternoon Mr. Prince. I'm special agent Roberts, and this is special agent Chang."

They pulled the two chairs from under the table, sat down, and agent Chang opened the file. Lee glanced and saw surveillance photos of Ashtiyani.

"So, what's the problem, and why do you have pictures of my executive?"

"Do you mind if we record this meeting?" agent Roberts asked.

"No, I don't mind. I just need to know what's going on."

"Sure, we understand. Today is Tuesday October 1st, 2019, 9:43 a.m. Mr. Prince, how long has CYGNUS Investments been in business?"

"A little over two years."

"And the board members are: yourself, Nicole Fitzpatrick, Jahi Davis, and Ashtiyani

Salman correct?"

"Yes, that's right."

"Mr. Prince, what are Ms. Salman's responsibilities at CYGNUS Investments?"

"She's responsible for managerial accounting of all CYGNUS' financial records."

"Is she authorized to sign checks, prepare the vouchers, record disbursements, as well as post to accounts payables and general ledgers?"

"Yes."

"Mr. Prince, we were able to obtain a warrant to look at CYGNUS Investments' financial records. We also subpoenaed the firm's tax records because of an investigation we're conducting on a Palestinian humanitarian organization that we believe to be a front for the terrorist group Hamas."

Lee jerked his head back. "What! That's ridiculous, what does that have to do with

CYGNUS Investments?"

"Well sir, while investigating that organization our counter intelligence terrorist taskforce discovered wire transfers from CYGNUS Investments."

"Mr. Prince," agent Chang interjected, "we have also been monitoring Ms. Salman's social media activities and have found very concerning content. What do you know about her connection to Palestine?"

"I don't get involved in her personal life. But to answer your question, nothing."

"We found that last year's tax filings for CYGNUS Investments show an $800,000 dollar write off as a charitable donation to the Fakka Foundation," agent Chang said.

"My firm contributes to several organizations that have legitimate causes. What does that prove?"

"Okay Mr. Prince, we are going to conclude this interview, but we'll be in contact with you as we move forward in our investigation," agent Roberts said before turning off the recorder. Agent Chang closed the file.

"So when can I get my computer drives back? Because without them my business operations are suffering."

"We will notify you," agent Chang said before he opened the door.

They all left the interview room and Lee exited the building. He looked up at the sky, then his phone rang. "Hello, what's up Percilla?"

"Lee, h… he's gone!" she cried. "Who's gone?"

Her voice was shaking. "Mr. Priest!"

"Calm down, what do you mean he's gone?"

"When I got home about ten minutes ago, I walked by Mr. and Mrs. Priest's bedroom and heard Mrs. Priest crying. So I knocked on the door before opening it and Mrs. Priest was sitting on her bed. I asked her if she was alright and she told me Mr. Priest's clothes were gone and he withdrew every penny from their bank account."

"What! Has anyone else seen him?"

"No Lee, no one has seen him, including his employees."

"Well, let me call you once I get back to my office. I just got done talking to Homeland

Security."

Lee spotted a taxi and flagged it down. When he returned to his office building and walked through the rotating doors into the lobby, Nicole was waiting for him. She scurried across the tile floor in his direction. "Lee, it's Ashtiyani," she uttered in a low voice. "She sent me a text a few minutes ago saying she has the solution to all CYGNUS' problems, and not to worry, she'll be out the way."

"What the hell does that mean?"

"I don't know."

Lee took a deep breath. "Do you know where she is?"

"No."

"Well, just keep trying to call her. I'll call from my number to see if she picks up." They walked to the elevator and Lee dialed Ashtiyani only to get her voicemail. When they reached their floor, Lee went into his office and Jahi was sitting in his chair.

"Hey unc."

"What are you doing in here?" Lee took off his jacket and hung it on the coat rack.

"I have a surprise."

"A surprise? I don't know if I can handle another surprise."

"This is some good news unc. My alma mater invited me to be a guest speaker to their business students."

"That is good news for a change. So, when is it?"

"This Friday afternoon at 1'O'clock in USC's auditorium."

"What are you going to speak about?"

"Not sure yet, but it'll be good."

"I know it will."

Lee dialed Ashtiyani again with no answer, and Jahi rose out of his chair. "Unc, everything alright?"

"Yeah, I'm just trying to reach Ashtiyani."

"Alright, I have work to do. So if you need me I'll be at my cubical. What did Homeland Security say about giving our computers back?"

"They'll let me know."

"That's crazy unc, but everything will turn out alright. If I see or hear anything from

Ashtiyani I'll let you know."

When Jahi left Lee sat in his chair and faced the window to look outside, hoping to find some semblance of peace. He leaned back, took a deep breath, and heard his office door open again. The unexpected sweet scent of Coco Mademoiselle filled his nostrils so he turned around.

"Jessica."

"Hi Lee."

"What brings you to L.A.?"

CHAPTER 13

Yusuf sat in the T.V. room of the prison watching Jim Cramer's Mad Money and looking at stock charts in the Investor's Business Daily newspaper when Hakeem walked in holding a Holy Qur'an, and sat across the table. "Salaam Alaikum brotha."

"What up bro?" Yusuf replied.

"I see you stay on them stocks, don't you?"

"I'm just puttin' a watch list together, because some of these companies are presenting buy opportunities."

"Brotha, I've always been curious as to how you know what companies to invest in, because you've made quite a bit of money since we've known each other."

"Well bro, I use a strict criterion. I first make sure the company grew its quarterly earnings over the past four quarters above 30 percent, the higher the better. Then the company's annual earnings growth over the past three years has to be at least 30 percent as well."

"So that's how you know?"

"Naw, it's more to it than that. I also look for any new innovations or products. Then I like to see that there is strong demand for the stock and the company is a leader in its industry. I want to also see that institutions such as mutual funds, hedge funds, banks, and insurance companies are acquiring the stock. Because those are the big players that create 80 percent of the market movement, buying and selling thousands, hundreds of thousands, and millions of shares."

"Brotha, I am amazed at how consistent you've been over the years."

"Bro, this has pretty much been my life in here for the past eight years ever since my relative told me to get on this, back when he was still in college."

"So that's how you got started?"

"Yep, and now my relative has made it happen in the industry with his own investment company. So I'm steppin' right into an analyst position."

Hakeem pointed to the sky. "If that aint a blessing from Allah, I don't know what is."

"Yeah bro, I'm truly fortunate. And on the same note, my son Jahi is going to give an economics lecture at USC in a few days."

"That's excellent my brotha, ya'll doin' it big."

Hakeem was serving a 96 month sentence for bank fraud and was to be released soon. He and Yusuf had become very close over the six years they'd been together and Hakeem would always tell Yusuf that God had a plan for him. Yusuf reflected to when he and Hakeem became friends.

* * *

It had been four months since Yusuf and Hakeem first met, when Yusuf was called to the

Chaplain's office. Chaplain Santiago saw Yusuf through the window and got up to open the door. "Hello Mr. Davis, please come in and have a seat."

Yusuf looked confused. "What's up, why did you call for me?"

"Mr. Davis, I'm sorry to inform you that your mother was killed last night."

Yusuf sprung out of the chair. "What! What do you mean my mother was killed?"

"Sir, I'm sorry, an attacker tried to rob her at gun point. She fought back and was shot in the chest."

Yusuf fell back into the chair and leaned over. He put his hands over his face. "Did they catch who did it," he sobbed.

"I don't believe so Mr. Davis, would you like to call any of your family?"

"Naw," Yusuf sniffled. "I'll call on my own phone later, but thanks."

A month had passed since Yusuf received the news about the death of his mother. He and Hakeem were walking the track around the recreation field and Hakeem took a pair of black Ray-ban sunglasses out of his pocket to protect his eyes because of a recent cataract surgery.

"Brotha Yusuf, I know you are fighting demons right now, but Allah has a plan for you." "Hakeem, no disrespect man, but if there really was a God like you say, then why would evil even exist? Besides that, why would a so-called loving God allow people to feel so much pain?"

"Brotha Yusuf, when your original nature senses danger it rushes to your aid. When a person is pressed by hardships and overwhelming problems, and the material factors turn their back on him, and he has no access to any of the resources of life and is drowning in a state of confusion, and death is but one step away, then an inward motive guides him instinctively to a non-material source of support."

"Man, that sounds good. But there are churches and mosques all around my city and niggas…excuse me, brotha's be getting' killed all the time."

"Brotha, if you were to look carefully, you'd see that the evil of things is not a true attribute, but a relative one. Firearms in the hands of your enemy is an evil for you, but firearms in your hands is an evil for your enemy. But set aside you and your enemy, firearms in themselves are neither good nor bad."

"Both sides of the wars are sick of burying family and friends, so why does it continue?"

"The course of nature is mathematical. Its system was established in such a way so as to not answer all our needs. We, however, wish to fulfill all our countless desires without encountering the least hindrance, and the forces of nature do not answer the limitless wishes we cherish, wishes which are in any event worthless from the point of view of our essential nature. Nature pays no attention to our desires and refuses to submit to our wants. So when we encounter unpleasantness in our lives, we become unjustifiably upset and we term the causes of our discomfort as evil."

Yusuf looked up at the white cloud shapes of a horse and dolphin. "That makes sense I guess."

The two continued to walk the track until it was time for Hakeem to make one of his daily prayers, so they went back to their housing location.

* * *

"Davis, 04357-212, report to the case manager's office," the intercom blared.

Yusuf got up from the table and folded his newspaper. "I'll see you in a minute, let me go see what this is about," he told Hakeem.

"Alright brotha, salaam."

Yusuf left the T.V. room and went down the hall to his case manager Ms. Wilkin's office.

She saw him through the window and waved for him to come in. "Have a seat Mr. Davis."

"How you doin' Ms. Wilkins?"

"I'm fine, thank you. I have your release papers and conditions of parole here for you to sign."

"I'm most definitely ready to sign my life away from here," Yusuf smiled.

Ms. Wilkins pointed to the bottom line. "Right there next to the x."

Yusuf's heart sped up and his hand shook as he signed his name. "Okay, is that it?"

"Yes, as far as this is concerned. But the warden told me to send you to her office once you were done here."

Yusuf left Ms. Wilkin's office on his way to the administration build- ing. Once inside he showed his I.D. badge to the secretary and she placed a call, then motioned for him to enter the warden's office.

"Warden Atwood, you wanted to see me?"

"Yes Mr. Davis, please sit."

"Sure." Yusuf sat in a chair located on the side of the door and noticed the blinds were closed. Warden Atwood scooted her chair from behind her desk and got up to lock the door. She walked in front of Yusuf and stood over him. Then bent down and kissed his lips with hot desire. Yusuf stood up, grabbed her around the waist, and pulled her body against his so he could tongue her deeply.

Warden Atwood stood five-foot-six, 120 pounds with sandy curls to her shoulders, and brown eyes. Her skin was freshly tanned from her favorite beach in Venice.

"I miss you so much," she moaned. Their tongues danced in each other's mouths, then Yusuf broke their kiss. Warden Atwood continued to lean her head forward not wanting to stop.

"Wait a second," Yusuf said.

"Okay, okay," she whined.

"We need to talk business; you know I can't be in here that long today. All of the brass is here."

"I know, I can't help it sometimes."

"Did you check your account?"

"Yes, there was $40,000 dollars in it, what am I supposed to do with that?"

"Let me see your phone."

"Okay." Warden Atwood went behind her desk, pulled open the top drawer, and handed Yusuf her iPhone.

"¿Cómo estas my friend? Have you prepared that setup for me? You know I have to land in paradise. Okay good, I'll talk to you soon." Yusuf hung up and gave warden Atwood the phone back. "Take a picture of me."

"Who were you talking to?"

"Just please hurry and take the picture so I can get out of here before we draw attention to ourselves by me being in here too long."

She sighed before snapping the photo.

Yusuf grabbed the phone and sent the picture, then erased all the information.

"What are you doing?" she said.

"Don't worry about that. Now I need you to go to Union Station in Downtown L.A. tomorrow morning. Once you get there someone will call you at exactly 10:00 a.m. to bring you a passport under the name Dion Williams."

"Are you going to leave me once you're released?" she asked under her breath.

"No, I'm taking you on a trip to Puerto Rico with me. We'll take surfing lessons, take a zipline through Toro Verde National Park, then tour through El Yunque National Forest."

"Oh baby, it sounds like you've been thinking about these places for a while."

"I have been. We'll stay at Hotel El Convento, sit in Spanish hand-crafted furniture, and walk barefoot on Andalusian tiled floors, then we'll eat mallorcas with lechon at La Bonbonera. And at nightfall, La Placita de Santurce, a historic market plaza turns into an open-air street party."

"Baby that sounds like a lot of fun."

"To top it off. Since I miss the ocean so much, we'll go snorkeling in the mornings at a spot called Champagne Reef."

Warden Atwood smiled from ear to ear. "I can't wait," she said.

"I need to get out of here. You know what to do, I'll see you tomorrow evening in the dining hall, just give me a nod and I'll know everything is taken care of."

"Okay." Yusuf kissed her on the lips before he left.

Hakeem met Yusuf on the sidewalk. "What's up brotha, everything alright?"

"I'm good man, I had to go to the top with my paperwork issue that my caseworker seemed to have a problem with."

"Is everything straightened out now?"

"Yeah, after I put my lawyer on 'em." They both laughed.

The next morning Yusuf walked in the television room with newspaper and coffee in hand, when he heard over the speaker system: "Davis, 04357-212 report to visitation for a legal visit." He turned around to take the coffee and newspaper back to his cell, irritated his cup would be cold once he returned. On his way to the visitation building he wondered why his lawyer would come to see him without notice.

When Yusuf walked through the doors there were two Caucasian men sitting at a table with a brown file on top of it. The corrections officer asked Yusuf for his I.D. and pointed in the direction of the two men. One of them was in his mid '50s with salt-and-pepper hair, and the other looked in his early '30s with black hair slicked back. Yusuf immediately noticed the Los Angeles, California Homicide Detective badges they wore around their necks.

"Mr. Yusuf Dwight Davis, federal number 04357-212?" the older detective asked.

"Yeah, that's me."

"Could you please have a seat, sir? I'm detective Harris and this is detective Stone. We are homicide detectives with the Los Angeles County Sheriff's Department investigating a cold case that occurred approximately 25 years ago."

"Why are you talkin' to me, I don't know anything about a cold case."

"Well Mr. Davis, we got an anonymous tip along with DNA that was entered into the inmate database that came back with a hit on you," The younger detective said.

"What?" Yusuf sprung out of the chair. "A DNA hit! Look, whatever you have to say you can contact my lawyer, because this little meeting here is over."

Yusuf walked away from the table.

"We'll see you again soon Mr. Davis," the older detective said before Yusuf opened the door to leave the building.

* * *

Three sets of skeletal remains were found in a shallow grave in the South Central neighborhood of 76th and Broadway. The small red brick house was purchased by a new owner who decided to build a half-court basketball rim for his two sons. When digging to prepare the foundation, he found human remains.

The authorities were notified, and the Los Angeles County Sheriff's Department sent homicide detectives along with forensic science anthropologists to secure the crime scene, scour for evidence, and excavate the bones. Investigators found pieces of duct tape and a cigarette butt. They concluded that the victims were naked when placed into the grave because no clothes were found.

At the L.A. County Forensic Lab, the bones were examined, and all three skulls had two bullet entries to the back of them. The teeth were cross-referenced against any possible dental records for identification, and the cigarette butt was sent to the California Bureau of Investigations lab for DNA extraction.

After approximately two weeks, during which the news of the discovery reached the public, a tipster phoned in with a name. When the lab results of the DNA came back and ran through the inmate database, there was a hit on a Yusuf Dwight Davis. The name given by the anonymous tipster.

CHAPTER 14

Back in Arizona it was a hot summer evening as the sun set at Sacaton Flats in Gila River.

Percilla was surrounded by her Pima-Maricopa Indian community to celebrate the O'odham New Year, which is the new moon of the summer solstice. She needed to clear her mind from what was going on at home with Mr. Priest, and there was no better way than to be around family and culture.

The orange full moon filled the sky as the night started off with Percilla and other women gathered in the middle of the dance circle to lead off the singing with all sister tribes from Salt-River, Tohono O'odham, and Ak-Chin. The women from every tribe wore their own unique traditional dress as they performed the swing and basket dances. Percilla wore a royal purple muslin two-piece wraparound skirt embroidered with Southwest Indian designs, and an aqua beaded necklace with a big sea shell in the center.

The white strip separated the darkness from pre-sunrise's violet by the time the festivities got over and Percilla got in her car to leave. On her way home she stopped at 7-Eleven to get gas. After she slid her debit card in the reader and grabbed the pump, a black van from the 1990s with dark-tinted windows parked on the side of her. Percilla didn't notice the driver get out. When she turned around to secure the pump she was grabbed from behind and a chloramine-soaked towel was pressed against her nose and mouth. Percilla struggled, became light-headed, then everything went dark. The perpetrator slid open the side door and quickly dragged her inside the vehicle. After slamming the door shut the kidnapper jumped in the driver's seat and screeched away. He drove to a remote area in an alley, zip-tied Percilla around her wrists and ankles, blindfolded her, and shoved a sock in her mouth that was secured with duct tape around her head.

* * *

Meanwhile, back in Los Angeles Jessica stood in Lee's office. "So, why didn't you just call me?" Lee asked.

"Because I wanted to talk to you in person," Jessica replied.

"Okay, about what?"

"Can we have some privacy?"

"Of course." Lee got up from his desk and told Nicole they were not to be disturbed. He closed the door and pulled down the blinds. "Jessica is everything alright?"

Jessica sat down. "I came to tell you that I'm going to Puerto Rico to have the baby."

"Puerto Rico. Why?"

"Because I want my baby to be born on my home island. I talked with my father about it and he agreed."

"So, you're saying that the only way I'll see you before the baby is born, is I'll have to fly out to Puerto Rico?"

"I didn't think you would mind if I left."

"Why would you think that?"

"I'm sure you'll be fine."

"What do you mean by that?"

"My flight leaves LAX to La Guardia in the morning."

"How can I get you to stay here in L.A. with me?"

Jessica stood to leave, and Lee went to hug her. She leaned back and turned her face away. "I have to go."

"It's like that? That's cold."

Jessica glanced down at Lee's crotch. "I'm sure the desert will keep you warm."

"The desert?" Lee looked at Jessica sideways.

"Well, do you need anything?"

"No, I'm fine." Jessica turned and walked out without even a glance back.

Nicole rushed in behind her. "Oh my God, Lee look." She showed Lee a newsfeed on her phone.

KTLA reported at 2:00 a.m. that a car was found in the warehouse district smoldering with a burned corpse inside. A witness told authorities he noticed black smoke when he was walking by and smelled an unbearable stench. Once a fire crew arrived, they discovered a charred cadaver in a mango colored BMW, and so the detectives and the Los Angeles Sheriff's forensics unit was called to the scene.

When investigators approached the driver's side they were immediately overwhelmed by the odor of burnt flesh and gasoline. The body was removed and placed in a body bag. The vehicle was hoisted onto a tow truck and hauled in to be analyzed.

At the lab medical examiners concluded that the body was burned too badly for fingerprints while an odontologist examined the teeth so they could be compared to any dental records. Around the neck of the victim was a burned gold necklace with a circular wire trinket, and the car was registered to Ashtiyani Salman of Torrance, California.

Lee stared in disbelief at what he was seeing on the screen. "This has to be a joke," he said under his breath.

"Lee, Lee," Nicole called. He snapped out of the daze, looked up, and took a deep breath. "Should we call downtown?" she asked.

"I guess so. Let them know we'll provide any information they need."

Nicole shook her head. "This is unbelievable."

"I need to be alone for a minute so I can wrap my head around this," Lee said.

"Are you going to be okay?"

"Yeah, I'll be alright."

Nicole left and Lee got up to pace in front of the window. He gazed at the powder-blue sky that was highlighted with an orange tint. How could all these tribulations be happening, he thought. Ashtiyani was his trusted partner and friend who was there from the very beginning. She played a pivotal role in the successful launch of CYGNUS Investments. The weight of the world was bearing down on Lee and he became psychologically paralyzed. There was a knock on the door. "Who is it?"

"Mr. Prince?"

"Yes, come in. How can I help you?"

"Sir, I have certified mail for you," the postal worker said. Lee signed the ledger and was given an envelope addressed from the Securities and Exchange Commission. He got a letter opener, sliced through the top of the envelope, and took out a piece of paper. It was a cease and desist order signed by U.S. Federal Judge Henry Gates stating that CYGNUS Investments must suspend all trading and account management activities by the close of business on Friday. The notice advised to direct any inquiries to Homeland Security attorney Geoffrey Crabtree.

Lee slapped the notice on top of his desk. "Fuck!" His phone vibrated and flashed a picture of Percilla's face. "Hello, hey Percilla."

"Is this Lee Prince?" a male voice on the other end asked that sounded like Darth Vader.

"Yes, who is this?"

"Listen carefully, because I'm only going to say this once. In five minutes I am going to send you some account numbers to deposit $1 million dollars into. You have by the end of today or Percilla's body will be found in the Arizona desert."

The caller was talking through some type of voice altering machine.

"Who the fuck is this playin' on my damn phone?"

"I assure you this is no game."

"How do I know this is real? Let me talk to Percilla."

The phone went silent for a few seconds.

"Lee," Percilla's voice trembled.

"Percilla, what's going on? Are you okay?"

Percilla's sobs faded to the background.

"Now, like I said, you have by the end of the day. And if police are called, she's dead."

The kidnapper hung up.

"Hello, hello. Shit!" Lee rubbed his bald head and let out a long sigh.

Nicole returned. "Detectives said we can go down there today. Lee are you okay?"

"I heard you."

"So when do you want to go?"

Lee's phone flashed a text from Percilla's number and he opened the message which were account numbers. "I have to take care of something first, I'll let you know. Please excuse me."

"Alright, are you sure you're going to be okay?" "I'm fine. Where is Jahi?"

Nicole looked at her watch. "He hasn't come in yet, but he should be here in about 15 or 20 minutes."

Nicole left and closed the door. Lee sat in his chair facing the computer, logged into his Bank of America account to transfer the funds, and realized they were international routing digits. He then picked up his phone. "Hello. Mr. Steinbrenner, this is Lee Prince. You said I could call you any time. Well, I have a problem with the SEC and Homeland Security. A federal judge ordered my firm to halt all trading and investing activities and I have a blank check with your name on it if you'd represent me in this matter, sir."

* * *

When Lee and Nicole left the L.A. detectives' office they had more questions than answers. The coroner wouldn't release Ashtiyani's body to her parents until the investigation was completed, so her father threatened a lawsuit based on Islam's tradition of a burial within 72 hours. However, the investigators did release Ashtiyani's personal items that were in her car.

Once Lee was back at his office he contemplated on when the right time would be to tell everyone about the letter he received. His phone rang. "Hello...okay." Lee quickly went out the door to Jahi's cubical. "Nephew, I have to go take care of something. Tell Nicole I went to run an errand," he whispered.

"Alright unc, you good?"

"Yeah, I'm straight. I'll see you later."

Lee left, got in the elevator and dialed LAX to book the next flight departing for Phoenix.

During the 50 minute travel all Lee could think about was getting Percilla home safe. When the plane landed, he rushed through the terminal to the arrivals lounge and waited like he was instructed. As people walked through the airport Lee scanned everyone, and constantly looked at his phone.

"Lee!" a female voice called.

Lee looked up from his phone and saw Percilla weaving through the crowd. He stood up and she jumped in his arms. "Are you alright?" he asked?"

"Yes, now I am," she sniffled.

"There's security, let's tell them what happened."

Percilla tightened her grip. "No. He said he'll hurt my family if the police were told."

"Where did you just come from?"

"I was dropped off in the parking garage and told to come in here."

"No one saw you?"

"No, he made me lie down wearing a blindfold then dropped me off and told me to count to one hundred."

Lee scrunched his face. "Did you see what he looked like?"

"Um, I did see out of a little space under the blindfold when I was lying down, that he was white with a bald head. But it looked like the back of him."

"You couldn't tell where you were kept?"

"No. All I know is I was in some room with a TV on."

"Let's get out of here so I can get you home."

They left the lobby and went outside to a taxi. During the ride Percilla snuggled under Lee's arm and laid the side of her face against his chest. They rode the entire way without saying a word.

When they arrived at the house and went inside, Percilla gave Lee a kiss on the cheek.

"Thank you so much."

Percilla went to take a shower and Lee went in the living room. He sunk into the leather recliner, took a deep breath, then slowly deflated his lungs.

Mrs. Priest appeared from the hallway. "Lee, hi hon."

"Oh, hi Mrs. Priest." Lee got up to give her a hug and could see the deep redness around her eyes from crying.

"What brings you to Arizona?"

"Nothing really, I just thought I'd pay a visit to see how everyone was doing."

"I'm doing as best as I can. I'm sure Percilla told you no one has heard from my husband."

"Yeah, she did, I'm sorry."

"My sister is flying in from New York tomorrow, so she'll be a big help."

"That's good, and hopefully we'll hear something soon."

"I hope so, but the FBI isn't really giving me much information."

Percilla came into the living room wearing a white T-shirt, black gym shorts, and her hair wrapped in a yellow drying towel. "Hi." She hugged Mrs. Priest.

"Hey hon, I haven't seen you in a couple of days."

"I was on the Rez helping with organizing for the festival."

"Okay. Well, I'll leave you two alone, but I'll be in my bedroom if you guys need anything. Nice to see you Lee." Mrs. Priest vanished down the hall.

Lee eased back into the chair. Percilla walked over to him and sat across his lap with her legs over the arm rest, and the two cuddled in the comfort of silence.

CHAPTER 15

When Lee returned to Los Angeles he went through the terminal and Jahi was waiting for him. "Hey unc, what's up, how was your trip?"

"It was alright. Mrs. Priest seems to be holding up okay."

"Did you find anything out about Mr. Priest, or where he might be?"

"No, still nothing."

"It's crazy unc, how you and the firm have to suffer because of all of this."

"I know, but I'll figure it out. Don't worry."

Jahi clapped his hands together. "On another note, guess what? I gotta show you something."

"Show me what?"

"You'll see. Come on let's get out of here."

They left the lounge headed to the parking garage where Jahi's pearl white Cadillac Escalade was parked. During the drive Lee stared out the window as they entered Brentwood. "Nephew, where are we going?"

"It's a surprise."

They turned onto North Bundy Drive and pulled into a magnificent three-level French chateau styled custom home.

"Why are we here, and who lives here?"

"Unc, this is my surprise, I live here."

"So this is your house?"

"Yep. Come on, let me show you." They got out of the SUV and walked to the front door. The house had a natural stone front courtyard with stone bench seats overlooking a square water bubbler. The house was smoke-grey with white window sills and white columns with extended height, that arched over the solid mahogany door entry.

"I like this nephew. Does your father know about this?"

"I haven't talked to him yet, but I'll tell him when he calls."

"I'm sure he'll love to see where he's paroling to."

They walked down the two-level natural stone-cut patio, around to the north side of the house's partially covered side patio with custom wrought iron railings. "Unc, the property is 7,000 square feet. Let me show you the inside."

Once inside the house Lee noticed the Concord elevator that serviced all three levels. "I see you went all out."

"Let me show you around." They went up the solid cherry-stained oak staircases to the top level as Jahi showed him the lustrous cherry hardwood floors. "Unc, the stone floor tiles on all three levels can be heated, as well as throughout the basement."

"That's pretty nice that you have all this."

Lee was concerned.

There were numerous LED pot lights, elegant sconce lights, skylights, and four solar tubes on the second floor. "I also had the entire house equipped with atmosphere lighting, Creston automated sound, and my security system hooked up to tablet-style touch pads."

Lee dropped his head.

Jahi led Lee down a hallway to one of the bathrooms with custom cabinetry and a bronze sink with marble counters next to a Toto toilet. They then went back down to the first level using the closet size elevator, to the kitchen with its Subzero stainless-steel built-in appliances.

"Nephew, how much did all this cost you?"

"I placed a bid and got it for $2.8 million."

Lee sighed. "Two point eight hunh."

"That's not bad unc, I got it $200,000 dollars under the ask. As a matter of fact, here's my realtor's card so you can call her whenever you buy another piece of property. She's excellent, plus she's the mother of one of my friends from college."

"Joetta Fields," Lee mumbled.

"We may see her later, she said she would try and make it to my lecture. I'll introduce you to her."

"So, what are you going to enlighten us with?"

"I'm going to speak about the economic aftereffects from the 2007 housing crisis."

"Why am I not surprised," Lee grinned.

"Speaking of which, I'm going to go upstairs and go over a couple of last minute details, then get ready. So make yourself at home unc, you just seen where the shower is."

"Alright."

Jahi had on a black Prada suit and white Polo button-up underneath, with black-on-black Santoni dress shoes. He was standing in front of a full-length mirror brushing his hair when Lee knocked on the door. "Come on in unc."

"Boy, you look sharp." Lee scanned around the sides and back of Jahi's head. "I see you got that fresh taper cut goin' on too."

"I'm just about ready." Jahi opened the watchcase sitting on his dresser and put on a black gator-band Cellini Moonphase Rolex.

Lee sniffed. "You smell good, what is that?"

"I'm wearing a new cologne by Armani called, Code Absolu. Are you ready to go?"

"Yeah."

* * *

Lee and Jahi arrived at the USC auditorium and a small crowd from the LGBTQ community was gathering on the sidewalk in front of the parking lot. It was a rally because of discrimination against a Muslim who identified as a male transgender who was being denied admittance into an Islamic fraternity. The protest was organized by the religious queer-positive group Al-Fatiha.

"What's goin' on?" Lee said.

Jahi focused in on one of the picket signs as he pulled into the parking space. "Civil Rights for Transgenders. Placement by Gender Identity Without Surgical Requirement is A Right," Jahi read.

They got out of the Escalade and went into the building where students were filling seats, and Jahi spotted his old economics professor. "Unc, let's go up front so you can sit near the stage." Lee took a seat while Jahi stood next to a business professor and administrators.

A middle-aged Caucasian woman named Ms. Parsons who had short black hair and wore square wire framed glasses, dressed in a crimson pant-suit walked onto the stage. "Good afternoon ladies and gentlemen. Today, I would like to introduce to our business majors and minors one of our own, Mr. Jahi Davis." The audience of nearly one hundred students applauded as Jahi went on stage to receive the microphone.

"Thank you Ms. Parsons, and thank all of you for coming. It is a privilege to speak to you today. My lecture is titled: 'Understanding the Past, Protects the Future.' You see, back in 2007 politicians had to show that our past economic crisis needed a solution but no problem even existed. The problem that didn't exist was a fake national problem of unaffordable housing.

When banks were allowed to change lending practices without regard, the housing market inflated into a boom; but inevitably went bust. Usually, housing affordability is measured in terms of a percentage of adjusted gross income, which is normally 30 percent to determine if monthly mortgage payments could be made. But there were many places here in California where it took half of a family's income just to possess a home. The subprime mortgage meltdown and financial credit crisis that led to the market collapse in 2008 could easily be traced to 1995, by the then current administration to push legislation called the Community Reinvestment Act of 1977, or CRA. The banks were mandated to make higher-risk loans in low income areas then they otherwise would have made. Failure to comply meant stiff penalties, lawsuits, and limits on getting approvals for branch expansions. In other words, our very government encouraged and coerced major banks to lower their long-proven safe-lending standards. We now know that most of these loans came with adjustable rates and many required little or no down payment, and those loans were packaged into AAA bonds and leveraged to other countries. The same administration that pushed the CRA also rescinded the legislation called the Glass-Steagall Act in 1998, which was passed through Congress after the great depression of 1929 to regulate the banks and financial institutions from being coerced into using the practices that created the housing crisis. So, as you can see, both political parties in Congress played a role in creating that great financial disaster."

Jahi continued with the economic impact on poor communities and how lingering effects remain, and the neglect of the recovery process by elected officials.

After Jahi concluded he looked to find Lee in the crowd of students, then called Nicole who livestreamed the event. Lee walked up. "That was excellent nephew."

"Nicole also said I did a great job. But Ashtiyani's phone keeps going straight to voicemail. Have you heard from her?"

"She's handling some stuff for the firm. But once she's done Nicole will show her the video," he lied.

"Alright, well, let's go get something to eat, I'm starving."

Jahi said his goodbyes to the business professors and faculty members before heading outside with Lee. They noticed the group of protestors had swelled. Charcoal clouds blew in, hid the sun, and the skies darkened as a storm approached.

"Jahi!" a female voice shouted across the parking lot. He looked up and saw it was his old friend from college with her mother Ms. Fields, his realtor. The clouds burst open into a downpour. Then, suddenly, a high-pitched roar of screams erupted. Jahi and Lee turned in the direction of the uproar and spotted a black Dodge Ram 20 feet in front of them heading in their direction, mowing down protestors. People were screaming and running when the truck jumped the curb.

"Nephew watch out!" Lee shouted.

Jahi was in shock at what he was witnessing and paralyzed in place. The Dodge Ram side-swiped him tossing him 12 feet in the air. His body landed with a thump on the tar. Lee rushed to his nephew and lifted his head off the ground. Blood ran between his fingers and trickled down his wrist.

The police had arrived earlier because of the growing crowd, so they were on the scene to shoot the perpetrator through the front windshield killing him as the truck crawled to a stop. Three protestors were murdered and five injured as rain showered over Jahi's face while he lay unresponsive.

An investigation revealed that the individual responsible was a white male in his '20s who was part of the white supremist group, War Skins. Detectives found a propagandist book called The Turner Diaries in the glove compartment. When the suspect's social media activities were looked at, there were posts of hate rhetoric found on the website WhiteSeparatist.com.

CHAPTER 16

From Denmark the small plane flew to Copenhagen. Once it landed there was a two- and-a-half-hour boat ride to a secluded area in the forest. The air was raw as early dusk loomed, and mud caked his boots as he tromped over the soggy forest floor to a simple wooden lodge located deep within the misty trees of Halmstad, Sweden.

With no electricity, bathrooms that were outhouses, and sinks that delivered filtered lake water from refillable tanks, this was an outdoor lifestyle he could get used to. There was an outside restaurant that was hidden deep within the woods surrounded by trees and illuminated only by candles, with tarps strung from branches to shield the kitchen from the elements. A bonfire constantly burned over which all the cooking, which served as a stovetop. It had a dual purpose because it also provided light for the cocktail bar and after-dinner lounge.

The food couldn't be refrigerated so the fish that came fresh out of the lake was prepared á la minute.

On his way to the sauna that floated on top of the lake, he ran into an old couple in their

'60s who were on a vacation retreat.

"Good evenin' to ya sir. We're the Göebbles from Norway, I'm Hue and dis ma wife Enis," the man said in his Norwegian accent. His grey hair was tucked beneath the sides of the white fishermen's hat he wore. And when he smiled his pale skin crinkled like worn-out leather.

"Hello, nice to meet you. I'm Freidrick Merkel from British Columbia," Mr. Priest said.

* * *

Gisselle was unaware the FBI had discovered her location in Switzerland and contacted Interpol, who put her under surveillance. In an attempt to find Mr. Priest's whereabouts, they monitored her phone conversations and Pristine Equities' account activities. One early morning investigators followed Gisselle to the currency exchange bank where she converted Swiss francs into Swedish kronas. They then learned she booked a flight to Copenhagen, so both agencies coordinated efforts with the Swedish authorities in case she met with Mr. Priest.

"Hi babe," Gisselle said as she carefully stepped out of the Jeep Wrangler that drove her to the lodge.

Mr. Priest held her by the arm. "You finally made it."

"The luggage is in the back, babe."

Mr. Priest got the two large suitcases out of the Jeep. "These are pretty heavy. Come on let's go to the cabin."

The two walked down a trail that ran alongside the lake. The mid-morning air was misty and the trees sparkled like jewels, the way the branches shone from the sunlight.

Once they arrived at the cabin and went in, Mr. Priest locked the door and drew the floral white curtains closed. He laid the suitcases on top of the bed, opened them, and saw Gisselle had brought the $1 million Swedish kronas like he instructed.

"Is that gonna be enough babe?"

"Yes, this will do. Are you hungry?"

"Um hm," she nodded.

Mr. Priest closed the suitcases and slid them under the bed. The two went back out the door to the lodge's restaurant to get brunch. They sat down at the handcrafted wooden table next to the bonfire, and the old couple who Mr. Priest met earlier was sitting across from them.

"Well, hello again," the man named Hue said. "Is dis here ya Mrs?" "Yes, this is my wife Hellen. Baby, this is Mr. and Mrs. Göebbles." "Nice to meet you." Gisselle and the Göbbles shook hands.

"So, what do ya do in British Columbia, if ya don't mind me askin'?" Hue was excited to strike up a conversation.

"We own a lodge similar to this one. We're looking to move to Sweden and searching to purchase another one while our son runs the other back home," Mr. Priest said.

"Oh, really. What kinda lodge ya own?"

"It's called Brew Creek. It's a quiet welcoming retreat south of Whistler with two guesthouses that are decorated in rustic style with post-and-beam timber frames and large stone fireplaces."

"Sounds great, how long ya gonna stay here?"

"Just a couple more days, then I'll talk to the owner of this place to see if they are interested in selling."

Hue raised his coffee mug and gave a nod. "Well, good luck to ya."

Mr. Priest and Gisselle ordered steak, eggs, and coffee. After they finished their meals Mr. Priest bought a bottle of red wine before they went back to the cabin. Once inside, Mr.

Priest lit scented candles around the room. He got two glasses out of the cabinet, poured them both a drink, as they sat on the bed. "Does anyone know where you are?" Mr. Priest asked.

"No babe, no one knows. I haven't told anyone."

"Did you get a different phone like I asked you to?"

"Yes babe."

"Okay, I'm just making sure."

Mr. Priest and Gisselle finished the bottle of wine and talked late into the afternoon. He leaned over and kissed her. "I was wondering when you were going to touch me," Gisselle whispered.

"You know I always desire you," Mr. Priest panted.

Mr. Priest palmed the back of Gisselle's head and ran his fingers through her blonde hair before gently kissing her pointed nose. He pressed his lips against hers and slid his tongue in her mouth and could taste saliva mixed with wine. Mr. Priest pulled the sweater she wore over her head and leaned her onto the mattress. After undressing the rest of her, he took off his own clothes and they crawled under the blankets.

Later that evening as the sun sunk behind the forest while Gisselle slept, Mr.

Priest eased from under the covers and tiptoed to the closet where he stashed a small pouch. He unzipped it, removed a medicine vial with a syringe, then looked over his shoulder to make sure he didn't wake Gisselle. Before turning around, he stuck the needle through the top of the vial and drew in a clear liquid that filled the syringe. He went back to the bed and slowly lifted the covers off Gisselle. Once her legs were exposed Mr. Priest stuck the needle in her right thigh. Gisselle jumped from the prick. "Oww! what was that?"

"Shh, everything will be okay."

Mr. Priest injected the fluid into her and Gisselle tried to move but couldn't. "What are you doing?" she slurred. "Why are y…" Gisselle's vision blurred, and she blacked out.

Before leaving the U.S. Mr. Priest obtained the clear crystalline compound from a nurse he knew that worked at Scottsdale Medical Center. The nurse told him it was succinylcholine, and it was used as a muscle relaxant for surgical procedures. She said if given in excessive amounts it would shut down the body's organs.

Mr. Priest leaned over Gisselle and laid his ear on her chest. Her heart stopped beating.

He covered her body with the blanket and reached under the bed to get the suitcases. Mr. Priest got his belongings making sure he left nothing behind, then got a towel to wipe down the room to eliminate any fingerprints. Before walking out the door he wiped the syringe and vial, wrapping both inside the rag. While he scampered the damp trail through the woods, he tossed it into the lake.

A screech owl shrieked across the sky in the distance.

"Freeze!" a chorus of voices shouted with flashlights behind guns.

Mr. Priest jumped. "What the…"

"Get on the ground!" demands were barked. Mr. Priest dropped the luggage and fell to his knees. He was rushed, shoved to the ground and handcuffed.

International authorities intercepted Gisselle in Copenhagen with the $1 million Swedish kronas before she could rendezvous with Mr. Priest. While in custody she brokered a deal with

U.S. and Swiss prosecutors to receive immunity from laundering, fraud, and conspiracy to embezzle, if she assisted in locating Mr. Priest. Agents had planted a tracking device inside one of the suitcases full of money which led to his capture.

When the Swedish police and FBI agents went to search the cabin where Mr. Priest stayed, they discovered Gisselle Helmsmith's body.

CHAPTER 17

The autopsy was completed and findings submitted to the medical examiner. Ashtiyani's body was X-rayed for any signs of external trauma, and a Y-incision opening the chest plate was conducted to inspect the internal organs. There were no traces of soot in her lungs nor in the nasal passage. The body tissue was sent to the pathologist and toxicology lab to test for any substances. The results were negative.

Detectives were baffled that the cause of death was undetermined because the report stated that Ashtiyani's death had to have occurred before the fire. It would have been unlikely for her to burn from an accelerant in a car while still alive without attempting to escape unless she was incapacitated. The position of the body indicated no signs of movement nor was she secured with a seatbelt, and both doors were unlocked. Investigators also found it odd that the BMW was parked in an open area on a corner where it could easily be spotted.

Detectives went to Ashtiyani's loft in Torrance to look for any clues that would explain the unanswered questions. They combed through all her personal items in every room. In Ashtiyani's bedroom closet there were barely any clothes and all her jewelry boxes were empty. Lying on the kitchen table detectives found a single obituary section from the local newspaper.

* * *

Meanwhile, Jahi was in the hospital lying in a coma. Lee sat next to his bed, eyes swollen from tears, and his soul blistered. Jahi's head was wrapped in bandages and an oxygen tube lodged in his mouth. The only sounds were the air pumping through the machine and the hypnotizing beeps confirming life from the heart monitor.

Nicole walked into the room with a bouquet of yellow roses in a glass vase and sat them on the small table next to Jahi's bed. "Hi Lee, has there been any changes?"

"No, nothing."

Nicole eased on the right side of Lee and rubbed the back of his shoulder. "He's going to be okay."

Lee dropped his head. "I hope so," he mumbled. Out the corner of his eye he noticed a figure and lifted his head. It was Percilla. He stood as she approached him.

"Hi. I took the earliest flight that I could, how is your nephew?" The two embraced.

"He's still in a coma. The doctor doesn't even know how long he'll stay in it, or if he'll ever come out of it."

Percilla wrapped her arms around Lee's neck and squeezed him. "I'm sorry." "Thank you. Oh, excuse me, this is Nicole. Nicole this is Percilla."

"Hello Nicole, I've heard so much about you."

"Hi, nice to meet you." Nicole gave Percilla a hug.

Percilla removed a necklace from around her neck that was made of brown nylon string with a webbed circle design.

"What is that?" Lee asked.

Percilla hung it around the vase of roses facing Jahi. "It's a dream catcher."

"A dream catcher?"

"Yes, in my culture we believe these catches all of our bad dreams."

"How does that help?"

"Bad dreams come with negative energy that weakens us, and we need your nephew to be strong."

"Oh. I just wish God hadn't placed this heavy burden on me."

"Lee, the creator that our people call I'Thor, has to place us into difficulties."

"What do you mean?"

"Think about it. Are there any life forms that come into existence that is exempt from struggle?"

Nicole pulled up a chair and listened.

"No, I guess not."

"If I'Thor created us to face difficulty, then a difficult factor is present that intensifies as we move closer to our ultimate goal…the difficulty factor is attached to everything of value."

"So, you're saying we must struggle toward some goal, but what is that?"

"Lee, without struggle we cannot bring out of ourselves that which I'Thor has deposited within us. And what has been deposited in us, is the potential to be one with Him. So when we face difficulty, and struggle, we are forced to turn to the creator for help, and on Him alone must we rely."

Lee glanced over at Nicole who was slowly nodding her head in agreement.

"I understand. It's just that I've been through so much. Now my nephew…I made a promise." Lee fought back tears.

"He's going to make it through."

"And I'm probably going to lose the firm I've worked so hard to build. I don't know what I'm going to do."

"Lee, your nephew is going to come out of this, and I promise you that CYGNUS Investments will be fine."

"How? You're always so optimistic. I may never get my license back, and the SEC might keep the firm shut down permanently. But none of that matters when it comes to my nephew."

"She's right Lee," Nicole said. "Everything will work itself out."

Lee faced Jahi, stood over him, and took his hand. "I guess you guys are right." Jahi twitched. "He moved! Call the doctor!" Lee shouted."

"Are you sure?" Percilla asked.

"Yeah I'm sure, go get the doctor!"

Nicole sprung from the chair toward the hallway. Then rushed back with the nurse.

"What's wrong sir?" the nurse said.

"My nephew's hand moved."

The nurse checked Jahi's vitals and I.V. "Let me just check his…oh, he's responsive." Jahi moved his arm. "See, I told you," Lee pointed.

"I'll get the doctor."

The nurse returned with the doctor who conducted a preliminary check to confirm that Jahi was out of the coma. The doctor told Lee, Nicole, and Percilla they would only be allowed a few more minutes of visitation.

Nicole pressed praying hands against her lips. "Thank God, that's unbelievable."

"The Great Spirit returned him," Percilla said.

Lee took a breath, then slowly exhaled, and a tear rolled from his eye. Percilla stood on her tiptoes and kissed him on the cheek. "I told you," she whispered.

"I'm so grateful my nephew is back." Lee's phone vibrated in his pocket. "Excuse me for a second…hello. Yes, this is he."

After a few minutes on the phone, Lee hung up and stared at Nicole, eyes wide with his mouth open.

"Lee, is everything alright?" Nicole asked.

"I just got a call from Liberal Insurance."

"Why?"

"They called to inform me that Ashtiyani took out a $1 million dollar life insurance policy with me as the beneficiary."

"Really. Why would she make you her beneficiary instead of her parents?"

"I have no idea."

"No pun intended, but you're no welfare case."

Percilla didn't say anything. With a slight curve at the corner of her mouth, she grinned at Lee with a look he hadn't seen before.

* * *

The strength of the sun's rays illuminated the cradle of an ancient civilization as the tour bus traveled the busy roads from the port city of Alexandria in the north, to the Giza Plateau. It drove through green farmland along the Nile River where such crops as rice, wheat, and maize are grown, which gave way to the rugged hills and gorges of the valley of the Queens in Luxor.

The bus left Cairo so tourists could see the Great Sphinx and visit inside The Great Pyramid before the sun rests below the horizon, in addition to exploring ancient Thebes before leaving the beaten path to ogle the soaring columns of the Temple of Khnum at Esna. The sunset was painting the eastern sky's canvas with an orange hue with the call to prayer blaring through the speakers from Mosque-Madrassa.

Later that night, after returning to Cairo to Oberoi Hotel & Resort, she stood on the balcony overlooking the great city, and the phone rang.

"Hello…thanks. I appreciate you for helping me wash Lee's hands Percilla. Now the firm will be okay. I'll see you soon. Goodbye," Ashtiyani said.

From MAIN ST.
To WALL ST.

INTERNATIONAL MOGUL

CHAPTER 1

Shanghai, China 12:02 a.m.

It was the Chinese New Year and Amanda Zhang hung upside down by a velvet rope tied around her ankles from the twenty-fifth floor balcony of the Ritz-Carlton in the financial district overlooking the Huangpu River. The cold air penetrated through her thin blue cheongsam from the winds that gusted and swayed her dangling body.

"Please! Don't kill me! I'm sorry!" she cried in the pitch of darkness. Flashes of light lit up her face from the crackling fireworks that echoed in the sky to drown out her screams.

"Me no play! You no tell me, you die!" Na Li eased her grip.

Standing behind Na Li was Sue Yuan with the slack wrapped around her waist. They had the lights in the hotel room turned off to obscure the view from any spectators.

"I don't know, I swear!" Amanda sobbed. Blood rushed through her veins that popped down the middle of her forehead.

"Me count one, two, three, and let go!" Na Li barked.

"Please!"

"One…two…"

"Okay, okay! 33, 21, 9."

"Did you copy that?" Sue Yaun said into the cellphone that lay face-up in the lounge chair next to the edge of the cement barrier.

"Just a second…okay, it's good. Bye Amanda," Yusuf chuckled.

Sue Yaun unwound the rope from her waist, Na Li released her grasp, and Amanda Zhang fell to the sidewalk.

* * *

The Los Angeles County District Attorney's Office was reluctant to file murder charges against Yusuf. Though the cigarette butt at the crime scene contained his DNA, there was no other corroborating evidence, nor any witnesses.

When the gates to the prison squeaked open Yusuf walked across the threshold from incarceration to freedom. The morning sun shone its UV rays on his face and he could feel the vitamin D soaking into his skin. He walked to the white Cadillac Escalade where Jahi and Lee were waiting. "Hey pops." Jahi embraced his father.

"Finally." Yusuf squeezed his son not wanting to let go. "You look good son, I can barely see the scar from your surgery."

"I'm straight, but I still go to doctor's appointments twice a month for check-ups because I get really bad headaches."

Yusuf turned to hug Lee. "Relative, what's up?"

"Man, it's good to finally see you out of that cage."

"Thanks for takin' care of my son all these years."

"That's my nephew, I had to."

"It's on now," Yusuf whispered in Lee's ear. They both laughed. Lee handed Yusuf an iPhone X. "Here you go."

"Thanks, relative."

"I see you finally let those French braids go and went bald headed like me."

"Shit, I didn't have a choice." They all chucked.

"I know you're hungry, what do you feel like eating?"

"I've been craving real Chinese lamb fillets with scallions, sliced in stir fried garlic, and glazed with sweet bean paste."

"Okay then, Chinese it is."

They all got into the SUV and left the prison grounds. Jahi got on interstate-5 and drove south until they reached Los Angeles' China Town. Jahi found a parking space next to a lively café and they got out and went to one of the many tables stationed outside in front of the restaurant and sat down. A waitress came with three menus. "Good morning would you gentlemen like anything to drink, or are you ready to place an order?" the waitress asked.

"Um, could we get some water please? And we'll be ready to order in a few minutes,"

Jahi said.

Yusuf scanned over the menu. "Let me see what they got goin' on here. Yep, they got what I'm looking for."

When the waitress returned with the water, Jahi ordered Yusuf and himself the Shangdong dish of sweet and sour Yellow River carp, deep fried and braised in wine sauce. "Pops, you're going to love it here."

"Lee, what are you gonna get? Since it seems ya'll obviously have been here before,"

Yusuf said sarcastically.

"Mam, I'll have the deep-fried bite sized sweet and sour spare ribs braised in soy, please," Lee said.

"You're soundin' real bourgeois right now," Yusuf grinned.

"What, me? Look at the word you just called me." All three of them burst out laughing.

A tear swelled in the corner of Yusuf's right eye from cracking up. "I'm so glad to be with my family."

The waitress returned with their plates along with three sets of chopsticks. "Would you gentlemen like anything else?"

"No thank you, this is fine," Jahi replied.

Lee and Jahi snickered as they watched Yusuf struggle to pick up food with the chopsticks. He tossed them on the side of the plate. "I need a fork."

"This is how you use 'em pops. Place one chopstick in the crook of your thumb and forefinger, support it with the middle and ring finger and keep it there with the knuckle of your thumb like this. See. Then hold the second stick like a pencil between the middle and index finger like this, but keep the lower stick stationary, with the tips even, and use your thumb as an axis."

Yusuf balanced the sticks between his fingers. "Like this?"

"Yeah pops, you got it."

"Son, you explained that like a pro. Is your mother half Chinese and I don't know?"

Yusuf joked.

Lee called over a young female waitress who stood five-foot-two, wore a red Chinese qipao with shiny black hair parted down the middle, tied in two pigtails. He asked her to bring a bottle of Great Wall Chinese red wine. When she returned with the wine and three glasses, she sat them on the table and Yusuf gently touched her hand.

"Oh," she cooed.

"Please excuse me if I appear to act inappropriately, but do you mind if I have your name?"

"My name is Amanda."

"Well, hello, nice to meet you, my name is Yusuf. I have to admit that the food here is excellent, and as long as you work for this fine establishment I'll continue to eat here just to see your smile radiate throughout this restaurant."

Amanda raised her eyebrow. "Well, thank you for the compliment." Her slight grin revealed tiny dimples.

"As a matter of fact, I would be honored to see how that smile glows in the dark. Is it possible that I may take you out for a drink one night?

"I'm sorry, but I don't drink."

"How about dinner and a movie then?"

"I'll tell you what Mr. Yusuf. You may meet me at the China Puppet Art Theater, Saturday night."

"Okay. But I must say, I've never been to a puppet theater, what is it?"

"It's a play with wooden puppets that involve elaborate and colorfully dressed marionettes. The fun is as much in admiring the craftsmanship and dexterity, then attempting to work out the plot."

"Sounds great. Can I see your phone so I can put my number in it?"

"Alright, excuse me I'll be right back." Amanda went inside the restaurant and returned with her phone.

"Oh, shoot. Son, what's my number?" Yusuf handed the phone to Jahi. "Sorry, my son just bought me a phone as a gift. Here you go, I hope to talk to you soon."

"I guess I'll see you on Saturday," Amanda said before she walked away to serve another customer.

"You most definitely will," Yusuf said under his breath.

"Dang pops, you haven't even been home 24 hours yet," Jahi smirked. Lee shook his head and smiled. "Yeah relative, I see you don't waste no time."

"I still have a few days it's only Monday, enough time to go shopping for my necessities.

Then I'll look for a house and vehicle sometime next week."

Jahi grinned. "Pops just let me play Uber for you for now. We don't want you to kill nobody."

"I gotta take the driving test over anyways."

They got up to leave the restaurant and Lee put two $100 dollar bills inside the menu and laid it on the table.

Five days had passed, and Yusuf stood in the full-length mirror in Jahi's house wearing a white Express jacket, white AG Green Label buttondown, white Nautica jeans, and black leather Mark Mason dress shoes.

Jahi knocked on the bedroom door. "Pops you almost ready?"

"Yeah, come in." Yusuf put on his black leather-band Tissot watch and saw it was 7:40 p.m. "POkay, I'm ready. I have to meet her in front of the theater downtown at 8'oclock."

Yusuf arrived in the parking lot 10 minutes early. A black Range Rover Sport pulled next to Jahi's Escalade and Amanda stepped out of the driver's side wearing a cherry red cheongsam knee-length silk dress with a slit skirt and Mandarin collar. She wore open-toe black-strap Versace sandals that displayed freshly manicured red acrylic toenails and smelled of Jo Malone London's Red Rose.

Yusuf got out of the SUV. "Have fun pops," Jahi said.

"Alright son, I'll see you later." Yusuf did a quick scan over Amanda. "Well, aren't you the bloomed rose after a light sprinkle with its petals glistening."

Amanda blushed. She put her keys in a handheld Louis Vuitton snap pouch. "Are you ready to go in?"

"Sure." They walked up to the booth where Yusuf purchased two tickets, and they entered the theater.

After two hours the two exited the building and went back into the parking lot to Amanda's vehicle. A slight breeze whispered, and the heavens revealed the big and little dipper affixed against the indigo canvas.

"Is someone going to pick you up?" Amanda asked.

"Yeah, I just have to call my son."

"Why don't you drive?"

"Well, honestly I just got out of federal prison the same day we met at the restaurant.

So I don't have my license yet."

"Prison? How long were you in there?"

"Over 20 years."

Amanda's eyes widened. "Wow."

"I hope that doesn't scare you off."

"No, you seem like a very nice guy. Plus, I believe most people deserve a second chance."

"Now that you know something about me, tell me about yourself."

"I grew up in Los Angeles, but my parents are from Shanghai, China."

"That's interesting. Do you speak the language?"

"Yes, I'm fluent in Mandarin."

"The reason I asked is because you really don't have much of an accent."

"It's because I was born in the States. But I visit China often, my father still has a house there."

"Oh, really?"

"Yes, he has a 20th-century European-styled mansion in Si Nan Lu."

"What do your parents do?"

"My father owns a firm called Zhang Accounting Services, and the restaurant where we met, is me and my mother's. What about your parents?"

"Both of my parents are dead. My father was stabbed to death in a bad drug deal, and my mother was shot and killed by an armed robber while I was in prison."

"I'm sorry."

"Thanks."

"So, what are you going to do now that you're out of prison?"

"My relative you saw me with at the restaurant has an investment company named CYGNUS Investments. I'll be an analyst there once I get my security license."

"What will you be analyzing?"

"Equities and different investment vehicles."

"How do you know how to do that?"

"I learned while I was in prison, where I also received my MBA."

"Impressive. If you don't mind me asking, why were you in prison?"

"I used to sell drugs a long time ago. But I no longer partake in that type of activity. I do feel that I was given an unjust sentence though."

"Why?"

"Because I've seen murderers serve less time."

"In America it's called the people's court, so I guess that means it's the people's justice." "Well, my people have been searching for justice for over 400 years, and their justice means 'just-us,' for them. So the only way my people will see any real justice, is through some type of revolution. Be it economically or politically."

"Have you ever heard of Confucius?"

"Yeah, he was a Chinese philosopher."

"In my culture we have a canonical book called The I-Ching, or The Book of Changes. He wrote a piece of commentary dealing with revolution. Do you want to hear it?"

"Sure."

"I actually have it on my phone." Amanda got her phone out of her snap pouch and brought the I-Ching up on the screen and began reading: "Abolishing the old. When the revolution tempest breaks out, faith must accord with it. Great success comes through justice. Revolution takes place not merely to overthrow the old, its purpose is to establish the new, and the new should be better than the old. Revolution does not happen by accident, there is always a reason. One can never create a revolution, and on the other hand, if a revolution is on the road, it can only be stopped by following the will of heaven and acting in accord with the wishes of the people. First of all, caring for and nourishing the people. The purpose of a revolution is not merely to overthrow the old, but more importantly, to establish a new situation and a better order. Abolishing the old is difficult; establishing the new is even more so. Both, abolishing the old and establishing the new need qualified personnel of extraordinary ability."

Yusuf slowly nodded. "That makes a lot of sense."

The two talked in the parking lot for nearly an hour before Yusuf called Jahi to pick him up. Once Jahi arrived Amanda agreed to another date before they parted ways.

"So, how did it go?" Jahi asked.

"Smooth as silk son," Yusuf chuckled. "Tomorrow I'm gonna need you to drive me up to Venice."

"Alright. But what's in Venice?"

"A warden friend of mine."

"A warden? Never mind, I don't even want to know."

Jahi shook his head and continued to Brentwood.